My Kind of Town

A Play by
John Conroy

chicago dramaworks

new plays. **chicago style**.

My Kind of Town (1ˢᵗ ed. 2015)
Copyright © 2015 John Conroy

For Colette, Matthew and Sarah

Acknowledgements

But for Nick Bowling and P.J. Powers of TimeLine Theatre, this play would be in a filing cabinet, unseen and unapplauded. They offered invaluable guidance and inspired editing. Ben Thiem contributed his keen eye, Nick assembled and directed a stellar cast and production team, and the TimeLine audience and supporters embraced the play. I'd like to thank the actors in particular -- Ora Jones, A.C. Smith, Charles Gardner, Derek Garza, Carolyn Hoerdemann, Maggie Kettering, Mildred Marie Langford, Mechelle Moe, Danica Monroe, Trinity Murdock, and David Parkes – who had great insight and tolerated many line changes. Lara Goetsch did a fine job promoting the play, Maren Robinson was a fine dramaturg and Juliet Hart has been a staunch supporter of the play as director of TimeLine's Living History Education Program in Chicago Public Schools. I owe the whole company big time.

Before TimeLine, there were others who nudged this play along. Steppenwolf Theatre chose the play for its First Look series. My hat goes off to them, particularly Jeff Perry, who was an early champion. And I would not have been able to put the play in Jeff's hands but for my friend and fellow playwright Dan Ursini, who kindly made that hand-to-hand exchange happen. Steppenwolf's Erica Daniels hired a fine group of actors for the reading, and many loyally stayed with me through several other readings. Kenn E. Head, Ora Jones, Erica Elam, Wendi Weber, James T. Alfred, Lia Mortensen, F. David Roth, James Farruggio, Jeff Perry, Dan McCarthy and Keith Kupferer all took part. I owe them big time as well. Ditto for directors Michael Patrick Thornton and Thomas Weitz.

Though I spent two decades covering the scandal on which this play is based, converting that journalism into a play was not something I considered until John Hancock came my way. Hancock, renowned theatre and movie writer, director and producer, asked me if I would join him for coffee to talk about the Chicago police torture scandal. At the end of our conversation, he said, "I think there's a play in this. Would you be interested in writing it?" Without that question, I would never have begun the process. He assembled a group of actors for the first reading of the play at 16th Street Theatre in Berwyn, where artistic director Ann Filmer kindly acted as host. Joanne Koch and other colleagues from Chicago Writers Bloc attended and offered valuable advice, and the family of Chicago playwright and activist Joe Savit later underwrote a reading of the play at a Chicago Writers Bloc New Play Festival.

And, as always, I got by with a help from my friends and family. Mike Lenehan, Mike and Betsy Miner, Alex Kotlowitz, Kathy Richland Pick, Christine Newman, my sisters Ann, Rita, and Mary Conroy, and Joanne Koch and the members of Chicago Writers Bloc all offered support and encouragement. And the Chicago Reader let me uncover the layers of the torture scandal over the course of 18 years. That too was a good, long run.

My Kind of Town was originally produced by TimeLine Theatre in Chicago, IL (PJ Powers, Artistic Director) in May 2012. The production was directed by Nick Bowling, with Associate Director Benjamin Thiem, Scenic Design by Brian Sidney Bembridge, Costume Design by Alex Wren Meadows, Lighting Design by Nic Jones, Sound Design and Original Music by Mikhail Fiksel, Properties Design by D.J. Reed, Video Design by Mike Tutaj, Dramaturgy by Maren Robinson, Assistant Direction by Spencer Ryan Diedrick, Stage Management by Ana Espinosa, and Production Management by John Kearns. The cast was as follows:

Rita Jeffries	Ora Jones
George Dawson	A.C. Smith
Otha Jeffries	Charles Gardner
Robert Morales	Derek Garza
Peg	Carolyn Hoerdemann
Maureen Buckley	Maggie Kettering
Ann Breen	Danica Monroe
Albert Jeffries	Trinity P. Murdock
Dan Breen	David Parkes

All productions of this play are required to include the following credit on the title page of the program:
My Kind of Town received its world premiere from TimeLine Theatre in Chicago, IL (PJ Powers, Artistic Director) in May 2012.

A Note from the Playwright

In the original production, one centralized table served as the center of activity in every scene – it was a table in a prison visiting room, in a police station interrogation room, in the kitchen of the Breen's and Jeffries' houses, in Buckley's father's pub, in Buckley's office (where it served as her desk), in the auto pound, and in court (where it served as the defense table and as the table in a waiting room off the courtroom). A second area with a counter, a coffee machine, and shelves served various purposes in homes, pub, office, auto pound, and police station. The design allowed for very fluid, centralized action as well as overlapping and shared space, keeping the various characters and families inhabiting the same world and environment. (In Act 2, Scene 7, for example, Dan and Ann Breen sat at breakfast at the same time that Albert Jeffries sat at the same table, eating his breakfast from a McDonald's wrapper, even though the two houses represented were miles apart.) The centralized table and counter in the rear, however, is not the only possible scenic design.

Also, in the original production, the part of defense attorney Robert Morrison was played by a Latino actor, who succeeded an African-American actor who had left the cast suddenly during rehearsals. During staged readings, the part was played by white actors. Some of the insults hurled at the attorney by his client (Otha Jeffries) varied according to what the actor looked like. In this script, all of those insults have been removed to give casting directors flexibility.

Lastly, this play is inspired by actual events. However, all characters, incidents, locations and timelines depicted are fictitious.

CHARACTERS

Otha Jeffries – Death Row inmate and torture victim, African-American

Theo Jeffries – 12-year-old son of Otha (father and son were played by the same actor in the original production)

Rita Jeffries – Mother of Otha Jeffries, ex-wife of Albert Jeffries, African-American

Albert Jeffries – Chicago policeman, African-American

Robert Morrison – Defense attorney who has taken on the Otha Jeffries case pro bono

Maureen Buckley – Assistant state's attorney (Cook County prosecutor)

George Dawson – Chicago police detective, African-American

Dan Breen – Chicago police detective

Ann Breen – Wife of Chicago police detective Peter Breen

Peg – Sister of Ann Breen

My Kind of Town

By John Conroy

ACT 1
SCENE 1

January, 1998. MORRISON, a lawyer, waits in a small interview room in a prison. This scene is resumed repeatedly in Act 1. Sound of keys unlocking the door. OTHA JEFFRIES, 31, enters wearing his prison uniform and handcuffs. He is furious.

OTHA JEFFRIES
Get your hands offa me you goddamn motherfucker. Goddamn motherfuck. Happy fucking New Year, asshole!

MORRISON
Hold on, Mr. Jeffries.

OTHA was expecting Leslie, his appellate lawyer, to be there.

OTHA JEFFRIES
What the fuck are you?

MORRISON
Take it easy.

OTHA JEFFRIES
Take it easy? You take it fuckin' easy. He does it every time. Let's see you try it, asshole.

MORRISON
Okay, okay. Point taken.

OTHA JEFFRIES
Point taken? Is that how they fuckin' talk now on LaSalle
Street?

MORRISON
Otha, I'm Robert Morrison.

OTHA JEFFRIES
Where the hell is Leslie?

MORRISON
Leslie did well, getting you this hearing, but she has a
caseload that would kill just about anybody. She asked me
to take it because I'm pretty good in a courtroom and I've
won some big appeals as well, mostly corporate work but...

OTHA JEFFRIES
Corporate work? Now I'm really fucked. Listen, asshole, you
don't know shit about this. She at least knew the score.
You're a three-piece suit motherfucker with a fuckin'
driveway in the fuckin' suburbs.

MORRISON
Otha, look, you're getting a good deal here. My firm is
committed to pro bono work, and we have more resources
than a public defender like Leslie. But if, at the end of the
day, you want to start all over again with somebody else,
you can decide to do that. Actually, I'll be deciding too.

OTHA JEFFRIES
What the fuck you got to decide?

MORRISON
You might be innocent, as you say, but you haven't got
much to work with.

OTHA JEFFRIES
What the fuck? You think I made this up? Me and all the other guys?

MORRISON
Mr. Jeffries, let's not waste our time arguing about what I believe. You gotta worry about what the judge believes. So let's just pretend that I'm the judge and you have to convince me that your story is true.

OTHA JEFFRIES
I don't do pretend. Haven't done pretend since kindergarten. Where the fuck did she get you?

MORRISON
Mr. Jeffries, I'll tell you what. Let's start with somethin' easy. Think you can answer a question without saying the word "fuck"?

OTHA sits in silence.

MORRISON
Alright. Where did you grow up? *(Silence)* What was your family like? *(Silence)* You play any sports? *(Beat)* You a Sox fan?

OTHA JEFFRIES
Fuck you. Where'd you grow up, asshole? You a Cubs fan?

MORRISON
Okay. I grew up in the Bush. Know where that is? 85th and Buffalo. Armpit of a neighborhood. Dad worked in a gas station. Got killed in an armed robbery when I was nine. Wrong place, wrong time. Mom worked in a beauty shop. Curl Up and Dye. D-Y-E, like you dye your hair.

OTHA JEFFRIES
I get it, asshole. You don't look like you grew up in the
Bush.

MORRISON
You don't look like you're innocent. Wanna convince me
otherwise?

OTHA JEFFRIES
I grew up in Chatham. Dad's a cop, and an asshole,

*ALBERT JEFFRIES, wearing police uniform, enters.
It's the morning he is leaving the house for good. He
brings his son breakfast. RITA JEFFRIES, his wife,
enters and stays in the background of the kitchen area,
watching.*

Never believed me. Left my mom when I was 13.

ALBERT JEFFRIES
So are you gonna eat that?

OTHA JEFFRIES *(responding as a 13-year-old)*
No. Can't buy me with some pancakes.

ALBERT sits down and starts eating the pancakes.

ALBERT JEFFRIES
Want me to drive you to school?

OTHA JEFFRIES
No.

ALBERT JEFFRIES
I've got my regular car.

OTHA JEFFRIES
No.

ALBERT JEFFRIES
I'm just sayin' -- nobody'd know.

OTHA JEFFRIES
Just tell me why you're leaving.

ALBERT JEFFRIES
Your mother and I decided it was for the best.

OTHA JEFFRIES
But why?

ALBERT JEFFRIES
Look, Otha, I'll still always be around. Be there Saturday, cheerin' you on.

OTHA JEFFRIES
Big fuckin' deal.

ALBERT JEFFRIES *(angered by the profanity)*
You mouth off like that one more time and I'll give you --

RITA JEFFRIES
If you're gonna leave, Albert, just leave.

ALBERT leaves in a huff. RITA comes to the table, picks up the plate and clears it away.

OTHA JEFFRIES *(responding as an adult)*
Better off without him.

MORRISON
Does he come see you now?

OTHA JEFFRIES
I don't want to see him and he don't want to see me.

MORRISON
We should talk to him - maybe he could help.

OTHA JEFFRIES
Fuck no.

MORRISON
Might've heard something. Might know somebody – a
disgruntled detective, somebody who could help us.

OTHA JEFFRIES
He's not gonna do shit. Don't talk to him.

MORRISON
Okay. Can we talk about what happened? *(Beat)* You admit
you stole those tires, right?

OTHA JEFFRIES
It was my birthday. Turned 19. Needed some money.

MORRISON
So you stole a car?

OTHA JEFFRIES
I didn't steal the fuckin' car.

MORRISON
But you were in the car.

OTHA JEFFRIES
I just wanted the tires.

MORRISON
For what?

OTHA JEFFRIES
LaToya wanted to go out that night, celebrate.

MORRISON
She your girlfriend?

OTHA JEFFRIES
Was.

MORRISON
Why this car?

OTHA JEFFRIES
It was there, in this lot – regular graveyard for cars. Guys stole one, they'd dump it there. I'd try to get the tires 'fore anybody else. Sell 'em to this old guy on Maxwell Street.

MORRISON
But your fingerprints are inside the vehicle, not just on the tires. You see my problem, Mr. Jeffries?

OTHA JEFFRIES
I see your God damn problem. You got to see my problem. Gotta pull the emergency brake or the car's gonna roll on you. That's why my prints are in the car.

MORRISON
So you're asking me to believe it was just bad luck that the car belonged to a drug dealer, really bad luck that he and his grandparents had just been murdered, their house set on fire.

OTHA JEFFRIES
I didn't kill nobody. I never heard of that nigger.

MORRISON
You didn't know him? Weren't you in the same line of
work?

OTHA JEFFRIES
You think 'cause I sold drugs, he sold drugs, I wanted to kill
him. That ain't how it works. He sold around 64th and
Morgan. I was three miles from there. I'm in competition
with guys two blocks, four blocks away. Three miles – might
as well be New York. I'm on death row 'cause I recycled
some tires.

MORRISON
So it's just a coincidence? You happened to --

OTHA JEFFRIES *(interrupting)*
I was hardly even sellin' drugs anymore. I was trying to
stop -- trying to get LaToya to stop cuz she was gonna have
my kid.

MORRISON
I'd like to talk to her. Where is she?

OTHA JEFFRIES
Dead for all I know.

MORRISON
Maybe she'll help. She's the mother of your son, right?

OTHA JEFFRIES
She was never no fuckin' mother to Theo.

MORRISON
Your mom and dad take care of him now?

OTHA JEFFRIES
My *mom*.

Pause.

MORRISON
Otha, we have to sell this story to the judge. If I'm havin' a
hard time believin' it, the judge is going to have the same
reaction, especially since you confessed. So I need you to
tell me about that night.

Pause. OTHA JEFFRIES gears up to go through this again.

OTHA JEFFRIES
I got home 'bout 7 o'clock.

RITA JEFFRIES enters and hands a business card to OTHA.

RITA JEFFRIES
Some police were here. They left their card, want you to call
them.

OTHA JEFFRIES
They ask me am I willing to talk to them 'bout some stolen
cars. I said yes. They came out to the house, talk to me for
about ten minutes, then ask if I'm willing to come to the
police station to continue the conversation with some other
detectives. I said yes.

MORRISON
Were you under arrest?

OTHA JEFFRIES
No.

MORRISON
Then why'd you go to the police station?

OTHA JEFFRIES
Nothing to hide. And I was tellin' my mom I wasn't dealin'
any more, and I wanted her to believe me. She wanted her
church-goin' boy back, and I wasn't goin' to no church but I
thought the least I could do was talk to some blue-eyed
motherfuckers about some stolen cars.

MORRISON
So you go to the police station...

OTHA JEFFRIES
They took me up to a room on the second floor. Table,
chairs. No clock, no windows. Handcuffed me and left.

MORRISON
What happened next?

OTHA JEFFRIES
After 'bout a hour, Breen came in.

*BREEN enters and confronts OTHA. He carries a file with
some photos in it.*

He asked me some questions about stolen cars. I told him
what I knew. Wasn't much. Then he starts talking about
murders, showing me pictures, people all burned up.

BREEN
Take a look at these, Otha.

MORRISON
Did you know them?

OTHA JEFFRIES
No, never heard of 'em, and I never killed anybody. I told
you -- I only stole some tires.

BREEN
Cut the bullshit, Otha. You set fire to this guy's house,
killed him and his grandparents, took his car.

OTHA JEFFRIES
No, I was home. I got a kid on the way, no way I'd do that, I
just...

BREEN
Your prints are in the car.

OTHA JEFFRIES
I want a lawyer.

BREEN
Your lawyer's busy.

BREEN exits.

OTHA JEFFRIES
And he just left. I sat there for I don't know how long, I
don't even know why the fuck I'm there. Cuffs are too tight.
I got to go to the bathroom, I start calling out, "Hello, can I
go to the bathroom?" *(Shouting)* "Can I go to the
bathroom?" Finally another detective comes in.

DAWSON enters and approaches OTHA.

MORRISON
What's this detective's name?

OTHA JEFFRIES
I didn't know, but my dad thinks it's a guy named George
Dawson.

MORRISON
What did he look like?

OTHA JEFFRIES
Big black guy, older. Glasses.

DAWSON
Do you want a cigarette?

OTHA JEFFRIES
I don't smoke.

DAWSON
You want something to eat? Water?

OTHA JEFFRIES
I wanna go to the bathroom.

DAWSON
Sorry, but they ain't finished interrogatin' you.

OTHA JEFFRIES
Okay then, I want a lawyer.

DAWSON
I'd like to help you, but I can't.

OTHA JEFFRIES
What's your name?

DAWSON
Listen, these other two guys are mean. Maybe you want to talk to me before they take you somewhere you don't want to go.

OTHA JEFFRIES
I don't have anything to fuckin' talk about, particularly to a peckerwood-lovin' asshole.

DAWSON
You sure now? 'Cause I know these guys. Next thing on the agenda's gonna be a trip to the basement.

OTHA JEFFRIES
Fuck you. These cuffs are killin' me, I don't know why the fuck I'm here, can't get a lawyer, you won't let me go to the bathroom, how much worse can it get?

DAWSON knocks on the door on the back wall. BREEN enters and takes OTHA off to the basement. Pause.

DAWSON
Worse.

SCENE 2

December, 1986, the second floor of a police station in Chicago, headquarters for the detectives working in the Area 2 violent crimes unit. A door on the back wall of this detective's bullpen serves as the door to an offstage interrogation room.

DAWSON is seated at a desk, typing a report on a manual typewriter. As BUCKLEY enters, DAWSON is doctoring his coffee from a flask he keeps in his pocket.

BUCKLEY
Excuse me, I'm felony review.

DAWSON
Yes, ma'am. I kind of figured that.

BUCKLEY
I'm here to take a statement on the triple homicide, the kid *(looks through her notes)...* Otha Jeffries.

DAWSON
You're in the right place, but they're not ready yet.

BUCKLEY
Well somebody called and said he'd given an oral.

DAWSON
It won't be long. I think they're just clearing up a few things
that have come in since. But don't worry. This is Area 2.
When the midnight crew says there's a confession coming,
you can take that to the bank.

BUCKLEY
You didn't work this one?

DAWSON
No, ma'am. I work afternoons. But the lieutenant don't like
the way I write the English language, so I'm rewriting a
report that don't need to be rewritten. Maybe we –

*ANN BREEN and her sister PEG enter, dressed up as if
they've been to a play and to dinner. They've had a few
drinks as well.*

ANN
Excuse me. We're looking for Dan Breen.

DAWSON
He's kind of in the middle of somethin'.

ANN
I'm sorry, I'm his wife, Ann, and this is my sister Peg.

DAWSON
George Dawson, pleased to meet you.

ANN
If he's busy, I can...

DAWSON
No, no. I'll get him.

With some reluctance, DAWSON goes to the interrogation room, knocks, opens the door a crack, and whispers to BREEN.

BUCKLEY *(addressing Ann and Peg)*
Hello, Maureen Buckley. Nice to meet you.

ANN
You too. Are you a witness or something?

BUCKLEY
I'm with the state's attorney...

BREEN enters, a little heated, but he cools when he sees his wife.

BREEN
Sorry.

ANN
We waited for you.

BREEN
Yeah, I caught this case comin' outta court and you were gone already. How was the show?

PEG *(sarcastically)*
You would have loved it. Lots of singing and dancing.

ANN
I thought since Peg is leaving so early for California you
might want to say good-bye. Might be a long time before
she's back.

BREEN
Nah. She won't be gone long. She thinks it's the land of
milk and honey, but it's full of fruits and nuts.

ANN *(admonishing)*
Danny.

BREEN
What? I'm not talkin' about anybody in particular.

PEG
Oh no.

BREEN
You'll see soon enough.

PEG
Danny, this might be paradise to you, but I'm lookin' for a
place where you can't ice skate in April and they won't let
you vote if you're dead.

BREEN
You'll see. You'll be back.

PEG
Wanna bet?

BREEN
Not here, no. Dawson here might bust my ass. Anyway, I
gotta get back. Good luck, Peg.

They embrace.

BREEN
You need me to make that ticket round trip, you call, any time, day or night.

PEG
Thanks, Danny, for helpin' me out.

ANN *(addressing DAWSON)*
Nice to meet you. Thanks. *(Addressing BUCKLEY)* Nice to meet you.

BUCKLEY
Nice to meet you too.

ANN *(to BREEN)*
See you later.

BUCKLEY
Have a safe trip.

PEG
Thanks.

ANN and PEG exit.

BREEN
Jesus. *(Beat)* Hello, Dan Breen.

BUCKLEY
Maureen Buckley.

BREEN
My wife's sister's movin' to San Francisco. She's in love.

BREEN *(continued)*
Guy's got the bent wrist, Cubs fan, you know what I mean.
I give her six months till she comes to her senses, back
home in a year. Howard's night off?

BUCKLEY
Yeah, I'm the floater tonight. I'm usually Area 4.

BREEN
Christ, talk about the bent wrist. Bunch of pansies up
there. 85 percent clearance rate last year? We killed 'em. 98
percent and we have twice the number of homicides. You
tell McCarthy that if they need help, they can always come
to us.

BUCKLEY
Okay, I'll let him know Dan Breen thinks he's a pansy.

BREEN
Well, for the sake of your own career, maybe you should
find a way to put that more diplomatically. Just tell him I
feel sorry for him.

BUCKLEY
Maybe I'll just tell him I had a nice conversation about
horticulture with the guys at Area 2.

BREEN
Jesus, Dawson, I think she's got our number. Hey,
Maureen, you seen this play, *Evita?*

BUCKLEY
No.

BREEN
My wife and her sister went to see it tonight, kind of a

BREEN *(continued)*
going-away celebration. Wanted me to go. It's got Che
Guevara singin'. I said, "You gotta be jokin'." I mean, come
on. Che Guevara shootin' somebody, okay. Che Guevara
singin', gimme a break.

Coffee's right here. We won't be long. Just pinnin' down
the fine details.

BUCKLEY
I hear his dad's on the force.

BREEN *(looking at DAWSON)*
Where'd you hear that?

BUCKLEY
They knew it downtown.

*BREEN begins walking to an empty desk, where he will
casually remove a plastic typewriter cover, fold it up, and
put it in his back pocket.*

DAWSON
Albert Jeffries. Good guy. Played ball with my cousin.

BREEN
His kid's trouble. Been after him for years.

BUCKLEY
Triple homicide, won't endear him to his dad.

BREEN
Yeah, we're doin' him a favor. Get the kid off the street.

BUCKLEY
So, am I gonna be here all night? I gotta let them know
downtown.

BREEN
Nah. You'll be in and out in an hour, your court reporter ever gets here. Dawson, show her the VIP lounge.

BREEN walks back to the interrogation room, the typewriter cover plainly visible to BUCKLEY and the audience.

BUCKLEY
Lounge?

DAWSON
He means the fire escape. Good place to get some air. Have a smoke.

BUCKLEY
I don't smoke.

DAWSON
Well, come out for the view then. You can see it all lit up.

BUCKLEY is only half willing, but she goes, and this conversation takes place on the fire escape.

See what I mean? You got the projects, Sears Tower, what more could you ask for?

BUCKLEY
Jeez, it's cold. Maybe I should get some of that coffee.

DAWSON *(blocking BUCKLEY'S exit)*
Made about six hours ago. Trust me, you don't want it.

The light in the interrogation room goes out.

First time down here?

BUCKLEY
Yeah.

*There is a painful shout. BUCKLEY hears it, as does
DAWSON. A few seconds later, the light in the
interrogation room comes back on.*

DAWSON
Where you from?

BUCKLEY
North side. All my life.

DAWSON
Where?

BUCKLEY
Around Granville and Broadway.

DAWSON
St. Gertrude's.

BUCKLEY *(a little surprised)*
That's right.

DAWSON
First communion with Father Sweeney.

BUCKLEY *(more surprised)*
Holy God.

DAWSON
High school at St. Scholastica's.

BUCKLEY
Whoa. I can see why you're a detective.

DAWSON
Did my field training there, back when it was called 41.
Probably you weren't even in school yet. Was there again in
'67.

BUCKLEY
My dad has a bar -- Leahy's? It's on Devon there. He
bought it in '69.

DAWSON
I know the place. Spent the night there once. January '67.
The big snow. Nobody could get home. Bunch of guys slept
in the funeral home there on Glenwood, but 'bout five of us
went to Leahy's. I wasn't gonna sleep with a bunch of dead
white folks I don't even know. Huge photos above the bar.
Daley, Kennedy --

BUCKLEY
Oh yeah, Stevenson. Truman. We had them up for years.

DAWSON
Leahy wasn't bad. Don't think he liked black folks, maybe
I'm the only one ever had a drink there, but that night we
were brothers. Great thing, snow like that. Hard as hell at
first, but then it covers everything up and makes people a
lot nicer, least for a day or two.

BUCKLEY
I never knew him.

DAWSON (brief pause as he recalls the evening)
Great night up there, all of us and Leahy. Maybe the best
night I ever had on the job. So, St. Gertrude, welcome to the
South Side.

BUCKLEY
Thanks. *(Beat)* I should probably check on that court
reporter.

DAWSON *(again, blocking her way out)*
He'll know we're out here.

BUCKLEY
You sure?

DAWSON
Yeah. Everybody comes out here.

BUCKLEY
Think they'll be a while?

DAWSON
Oh you know how it is. Always something you got to nail
down.

Beat.

BUCKLEY
I guess you grew up around here? South Side, I mean.

DAWSON
No. Wilmette.

*BUCKLEY laughs. The audience sees BREEN leave the
interrogation room and replace the typewriter cover over its
machine.*

DAWSON
No, we moved around. Now we're in Saint Sabina's.
Meaning we don't go to Sabina's, but we live in Sabina's.

BUCKLEY *(simultaneously with "we live in Sabina's.")*
But you live in Sabina's, yeah, I get it.

BREEN calls out to the fire escape.

BREEN
Ladies and gentlemen, we're done. We'll get him some
McDonald's, then you can have him.

*BREEN leaves. BUCKLEY moves as if she and DAWSON
will now be leaving the fire escape.*

DAWSON
Now, Maureen, listen here. Because that old white man did
me a favor that night in your neighborhood, this old black
man is gonna do you a favor tonight in my neighborhood.
(Beat) You ever float in here on midnights again, you want
to remember this fire escape. If Dan Breen comes out – or
any of the others – and they start rummaging around, that's
when you go out for a cigarette.

BUCKLEY
I don't get it.

DAWSON
Oh, you will. *(Beat)* Ever see a typewriter in an
interrogation room?

BUCKLEY
A typewriter?

DAWSON puts his finger to his lips, signaling silence.

DAWSON
It's cold. Let's go inside.

SCENE 3

Prison meeting room. The opening scene of the play resumes.

MORRISON
This George Dawson, he's not in the paperwork. The only detectives in the reports are Breen, Deluca, and Lieutenant Gunther. I know there were a bunch of guys who are supposed to have used the machines, but this is the first I've heard of an older black detective.

OTHA JEFFRIES
He didn't fuckin' use the machines.

MORRISON
And he didn't touch you.

OTHA JEFFRIES
Fucker didn't do shit. He just tried to get me to confess to somethin' I didn't do. And the reason you haven't heard of him is cause you're just like every-fuckin'-body else. Nobody listens.

MORRISON
Your mom listened.

OTHA JEFFRIES
Not at first. It took those anonymous letters sent to Calvin's lawyers -

MORRISON
About the machines. I read about them. *(Pulling out a copy of the newspaper)* This reporter thinks they were written by a cop.

OTHA JEFFRIES
They really got to her. All of a sudden, everythin' I been sayin', she starts askin' me to repeat it, she's writin' it down.

SCENE 4

April, 1997. Officer ALBERT JEFFRIES and his ex-wife, RITA JEFFRIES, in her kitchen. She's folding laundry. Some of the clothes are those of a 12-year-old boy. ALBERT sits with a cup of coffee. The same newspaper from Scene 3 is on the table in front of him.

ALBERT JEFFRIES *(motioning to the paper)*
When you start picking this up?

RITA JEFFRIES
Woman at church gave it to me. You saw it?

ALBERT JEFFRIES
A few guys mentioned it when it came out and I got one.

RITA JEFFRIES
You didn't tell me.

ALBERT JEFFRIES
It don't have nothin' to do with you.

RITA JEFFRIES
You don't see no connection?

ALBERT JEFFRIES
To what?

RITA JEFFRIES
Everything Donald Calvin says happened to him – it's the same thing Otha's been saying for years.

ALBERT JEFFRIES
Donald Calvin killed two cops.

RITA JEFFRIES
So he had it comin'?

ALBERT doesn't answer.

Albert, don't give me your silent treatment. Answer me.

ALBERT JEFFRIES
I don't know nothin' about it.

RITA JEFFRIES
You know some of them.

ALBERT JEFFRIES
I know 'em by name, not like you know somebody.

RITA JEFFRIES
Nobody? All the people at Area 2, you know nobody? .

ALBERT JEFFRIES
It was more'n ten years ago. Only guy I know mighta been there is George Dawson. He wouldn't know anything.

RITA JEFFRIES
You don't think he'd know if they got a machine that shocks people?

ALBERT JEFFRIES
Donald Calvin says they got one machine you plug in the wall, shocks people. You ever hear of a machine like that? Then he says they got a second machine, doesn't plug into the wall, you crank it by hand. What do they need two machines for? Case you want to shock somebody if the power goes out? Doesn't make any sense.

RITA JEFFRIES
Okay, so you're sayin' it makes sense if they got one
machine, but not if they got two? Don't make no difference
– one machine or two. A lot of guys said they got shocked.
Leslie says there's more comin' forward every month.

ALBERT JEFFRIES
They're all sayin' the same thing cause they hear it from
each other. Look I didn't come here for this. I came to see
my grandson.

RITA JEFFRIES
Oh yeah. I know. Plenty of time for Theo, no time for his
daddy.

ALBERT is silent.

Too far for you to drive?

ALBERT remains mute.

RITA JEFFRIES
Been there eleven years, you know he gonna die, and you
can't go see him.

ALBERT JEFFRIES
He don't want to see me.

RITA JEFFRIES
Maybe he don't want to see you because you won't go see
him.

ALBERT JEFFRIES
He don't want no part of me. Made that clear since he was
thirteen.

RITA JEFFRIES *(sarcastically)*
Oh, yeah. What happened when he was thirteen he turned against you?

ALBERT JEFFRIES
My leavin' had nothin' to do with him.

RITA JEFFRIES
You was ham and eggs. Mutt and Jeff. But no, we not good enough.

ALBERT JEFFRIES
Leave it alone.

Long pause.

RITA JEFFRIES
He'd be a cop today.

ALBERT JEFFRIES
Oh, yeah. Way he was goin', he'd be just like *(pointing to newspaper)* them. Fit right in.

RITA doesn't respond.

When Theo gonna be back?

RITA JEFFRIES
He got baseball. One day it takes a hour, the next day it takes three. *(Beat.)* What I don't understand is why you don't do something. Why don't you look into it?

ALBERT JEFFRIES
First of all, you know I'm in traffic. I never was no detective.

RITA JEFFRIES
But you can talk to them. I seen you. They like you. You make them feel like they the black man's friend. He didn't do it and you know it.

ALBERT JEFFRIES
He did plenty. You don't know the half of it.

RITA JEFFRIES
He sold drugs. Okay. I'm not blind. He stole tires. He shot his friend in the leg, but he was aimin' for his leg, he wasn't tryin' to kill him. Now all a sudden he gonna set fire to a man's house, steal his car, drive it to his own neighborhood, and then take off the tires in broad daylight?

ALBERT JEFFRIES
He confessed.

RITA JEFFRIES
After they covered his face with a plastic bag.

ALBERT JEFFRIES
No, no, no. After Otha says they put a bag over his face. Oh, he can talk the talk, I'll give him that. And I believed him.

RITA JEFFRIES
Okay, so he lied some times. You never lied when you were that age? You never lied to me? His story is the same as Calvin's, as a whole bunch of other guys.

Long pause. ALBERT prepares to exit.

ALBERT JEFFRIES
Where's Theo playin'? Maybe I'll catch the last inning.

RITA JEFFRIES
You can run, Albert, but you can't hide.

ALBERT JEFFRIES
What park?

RITA JEFFRIES
Jesse Owens.

SCENE 5

Prison meeting room. The opening scene of the play resumes.

MORRISON
So your son lives with your Mom?

OTHA JEFFRIES
Yeah. Sleeps in my old room.

MORRISON
Do you ever get to see him?

OTHA JEFFRIES
Once in a while. Round Christmas, usually, they make the trip. I think she's afraid I'll fuck him up.

MORRISON
And your dad's never been here?

OTHA JEFFRIES
Never. Haven't seen him since before I got arrested.

MORRISON
So he doesn't wanna help his only son? Or you don't want him to help?

OTHA JEFFRIES
I'm not his son, I'm his fuckin' nightmare, his biggest embarrassment. He wouldn't do a goddamn thing if I was

OTHA JEFFRIES *(continued)*
dyin' tomorrow. *(Beat)* My mother's all over the place, even
been on the news, all my father did was go talk to some guy
he already knew.

MORRISON
Is this the older black detective?

OTHA JEFFRIES
The guy my dad thinks is the older black detective.

SCENE 6

*May, 1997. ALBERT JEFFRIES calls on DAWSON, who is
now working in a trailer on the auto pound. DAWSON
doesn't appear to be too busy.*

ALBERT JEFFRIES
George Dawson. Albert Jeffries. I didn't know you were
down here.

DAWSON
Well, will you look what the dog dragged home.

ALBERT JEFFRIES
Long time.

DAWSON
It is. Don't tell me your car got towed.

ALBERT JEFFRIES
No. City's tryin' to figure out can we raise some more
money by towin' more cars, do we have the capacity to store
'em, the manpower, you know. Didn't know you'd be here.

DAWSON
Oh yeah. Been here a few years now.

ALBERT JEFFRIES
It's good?

DAWSON
Oh yeah.

ALBERT JEFFRIES
How's your boys?

DAWSON
They're good. You know they're both on the job?

ALBERT JEFFRIES
I heard that.

DAWSON
One's on a tac team in 15, the other's in 4.

ALBERT JEFFRIES
Cool.

DAWSON
And yours?

ALBERT JEFFRIES
Well, I got two girls now with Tamitha – you know I got
married again – and they're fine. Good girls, smart. Their
mother keeps 'em on a short leash.

DAWSON
With girls you've got to. Otherwise.

ALBERT JEFFRIES
And you know about Otha.

DAWSON
Yeah, I know.

ALBERT JEFFRIES
Haven't seen him in years. Rita says he's doin' okay. *(Beat)*
Well, it looks like you've got a good set up now. So tell me,
there room out here if they started towin' 30, 40 more cars
every day?

DAWSON
Room? Hell yeah. Not that I want to work any harder.

ALBERT JEFFRIES
So how'd you come to be here?

DAWSON
Jack Gunther. Wouldn't give me any homicides, so after a
while I said, the hell with this, complained to downtown.

ALBERT JEFFRIES
Shit. That took some balls, George.

DAWSON
Yeah. Was gettin' my courage from a bottle back then. So
Gunther started givin' me homicides all right -- I got every
bullshit case that came in the door, the ones where the only
witness says, "Didn't see his face or the license number,
officer, but I think the car was blue."

ALBERT JEFFRIES
Sounds like Gunther.

DAWSON
So my clearance rate went down fast. Then he had grounds,
busted me down to patrolman. But I ran into a guy'd
worked the auto pound, and after so many years on the
street it sounded fine to me.

ALBERT JEFFRIES
So you're livin' the good life. I'm glad somebody is. When you gonna retire?

DAWSON
Now why would I do that? This is about as close to not workin' as a man can get.

ALBERT JEFFRIES
Good for you. So you read that?

He references the same newspaper that appeared previously, though this is a different issue.

DAWSON
Nah. Last guy musta left it. Nothin' in it for a guy my age.

ALBERT JEFFRIES
You see the article about Donald Calvin...guy who shot Shanahan and O'Meara?

DAWSON
Yeah, I saw it.

ALBERT JEFFRIES
You hear anything, even a rumor, about Otha's case?

DAWSON
I remember hearing that he was arrested. That's about it.

ALBERT JEFFRIES
I was thinking everybody who worked over there must've heard somethin'.

DAWSON
Who worked the case?

ALBERT JEFFRIES
DeLuca, Breen, Gunther, and according to Otha, a black detective came in the room too.

DAWSON
Well DeLuca died about a year ago. Far as Breen and Gunther goes, I can tell you they're assholes, they had a reputation on the street, cut some corners.

ALBERT JEFFRIES
Well it sure looks like Gunther fucked up Donald Calvin, but Calvin had marks all over his body, radiator burns, scabs from alligator clips on his ears. Otha doesn't have any marks. Rita thinks they got smart. So it's Otha's word against theirs, and you know he loses that battle every time.

Beat.

DAWSON
What about the state's attorney who took his confession. You talk to him?

ALBERT JEFFRIES
Wasn't a him, it was a her. Maureen Buckley. She ain't gonna say nothin'.

DAWSON
She'd be implicatin' everybody – state's attorneys, some of 'em are judges now. The mayor. If this was going on, he knew, he was head of the office. Or he didn't want to know. Christ, she'd have to leave town.

ALBERT JEFFRIES
That's what I told Rita.

DAWSON
Yeah. *(Beat)* I'm real sorry Albert. I wish I could help you.

ALBERT JEFFRIES
Well even this helps, with Rita you know.

DAWSON
Must be hell, Albert, havin' two wives. How those Mormons
have three or four, man you couldn't pay me to do it.

ALBERT JEFFRIES
That damn woman has always been able to see me lyin',
could never fool her, she knew from the instant I started
sneakin' around.

DAWSON
Man, I hope you did a better job pickin' the second one.

ALBERT JEFFRIES
It's just Rita. Tamitha's fine.

DAWSON
Or maybe you're not such a good liar.

ALBERT JEFFRIES
Yeah. Maybe you're right.

DAWSON
Listen, you take care. Drop in again if you're down here.

ALBERT JEFFRIES
I will. Thanks.

SCENE 7

*Prison meeting room. The opening scene of the play
resumes.*

OTHA JEFFRIES
Asshole stood in the next room when they tortured me.

OTHA JEFFRIES *(continued)*
And now he pretends he wasn't even there.

MORRISON
Dawson might want to do the right thing, but he just needs
a lot of encouragement. Maybe I can give him some.

OTHA JEFFRIES
He ain't gonna say a goddamn motherfuckin' thing. He's
part of it.

MORRISON
(Pause) Otha, let's talk about the state's attorney, Maureen
Buckley. I guarantee you, when you get on the stand, the
prosecutor's gonna ask why you said nothing to her about
what happened.

OTHA JEFFRIES
The first thing she told me was she wasn't my attorney, she
was working with the police. And Breen was sittin' next to
me the whole time, makin' sure I didn't change my story.

MORRISON
Okay. What do you remember about her?

OTHA JEFFRIES
Not much. I only saw her for fifteen, twenty minutes. My
mom went to see her last year, prob'ly saw her for longer
than I did. Never thought she could do something like that.
Not in a million years.

SCENE 8

April, 1997. The office of prosecutor Maureen Buckley.
BUCKLEY answers the phone, speaking as if to a
receptionist.

BUCKLEY
Maureen Buckley. *(Pause)* She won't tell you her name?
(Pause) Is she crazy? *(Pause)* Well if she's so polite, why
doesn't she make an appointment? Do you think she'll
leave? *(Pause)* Oh, Christ, just send her in. Tell her I can
give her five minutes. Then call me back in five minutes so I
can get rid of her if I need to.

After a brief pause, RITA JEFFRIES enters the office.

RITA JEFFRIES
Mrs. Buckley, I'm really sorry to bother you, really sorry, I
see you in the papers and I know you're very busy and very
important. Thank you for seeing me.

BUCKLEY
Yes, ma'am.

RITA JEFFRIES
My name's Rita Jeffries. My husband is Albert Jeffries, we're
divorced, he's a police officer but he won't do anything. He
should be here.

BUCKLEY
What can I do for you?

RITA JEFFRIES
I'm here about my son. You met him once, you took his
confession about ten years ago, his name is Otha Jeffries.
He's on death row. I know you probably taken a lot of
confessions, and maybe you don't remember him.

BUCKLEY
I remember him, Mrs. Jeffries. Please don't tell me you're
here because you think he's innocent.

RITA JEFFRIES
Mrs. Buckley, I know you probably think I'm crazy, every mother thinks her son is innocent. But I know Otha was a criminal. I know he was sellin' drugs. And we wouldn't stand for that, and Albert put him out of my house. And I know he stole things and was in a gang and he shot that other boy in the leg, but he admitted all that. He admitted it to the police. Never denied it. But he don't set fires. He don't kill old people. You'll laugh at this, but he was nice to old people. Bertha Love, she testified for him, she older than dirt. And I'm just here because I looked at the police reports and I seen you were there the night he was arrested. And I can't really talk to the police officers, 'cause of my husband, and I thought a woman might understand, and I just wondered if you know if anything happened that night to Otha. I mean he says he got electric shock and suffocated. And in the paper it says that Donald Calvin said the same thing,

BUCKLEY
Mrs. Jeffries –

RITA JEFFRIES
...and I know I shouldn't mention Donald Calvin because I know he shot those two officers. But now there are other guys. And with Otha, the only evidence was the fingerprints in the car, the footprint at the house didn't match, the witness at the gas station said the guy had a moustache and Otha never had a moustache, and he couldn't pick Otha out of the lineup. And I'm sorry, I know I'm talkin' fast but I'm nervous bein' here and I don't want to take up your time and I just wanted to ask if you saw or heard anything in the police station that night.

BUCKLEY
Mrs. Jeffries, I'm sorry that your son put you in this
predicament. But I can't help you, except to maybe tell you
the truth, and that's that nothing happened that night. I
know the officers who were on duty that night. Breen and
Gunther, they are fine men. Gunther was decorated for valor
in Vietnam. Breen was a Marine, I've met his wife and kids.

*RITA looks into a file that she brought with her, hoping to
show something to BUCKLEY.*

RITA JEFFRIES
But –

BUCKLEY
And yes, Donald Calvin says he was tortured, and that
article makes it seem like the police are lying, but Mrs.
Jeffries, your son was in a gang and he probably heard that
story from them, a bunch of gang members conveniently
saying the same thing, but it won't work. It didn't happen.
And in a few months when the Police Board hearings are
over, I think you'll see that Commander Gunther is
exonerated and all of these stories will be exposed for what
they are – just something a bunch of guys made up.

Now, I've got a heavy caseload. I just finished a big trial, and
I'm way behind in all my other work. *(Pause)* I know it's not
easy with a son on death row, and I'm very sorry for you,
but I didn't put him there, he put himself there, and there's
nothing you can do about it *(beat)* except pray for him.

RITA JEFFRIES
Yeah. Okay. My pastor told me not to come, a waste of time
– but I watched you in the courtroom last week. I saw you--

*BUCKLEY's phone rings. She hesitates, then doesn't
answer. It keeps ringing. RITA talks right through it. After*

about five rings, BUCKLEY picks it up and covers the mouthpiece with her hand.

RITA JEFFRIES *(continued)*
--pleading with the jury on behalf of those dead black women from Englewood, lot of them prostitutes, people nobody missed but their family, and maybe not even them, and I thought...you're not...

I hope you think about it. For the rest of your life, I hope you think about it. I'm not sayin' you saw or heard anything. I'm just sayin' something was wrong, and now my son is gonna die, and that...

BUCKLEY
Mrs. Jeffries, I'm sorry, I have to take this.

RITA JEFFRIES
Well, Mrs. Buckley, thank you for your time.

RITA starts to exit. BUCKLEY calls out to her.

BUCKLEY
You're welcome. I'm sorry I can't help you.

RITA exits.

Maureen Buckley. *(Pause)* She's gone. Should walk past you in a second. Don't worry, she's not crazy. Just a little upset about her son. She thought I might know something about him. *(Pause)* No, you did the right thing. You can go home.

Have a nice weekend. *(Pause)* Thanks.

SCENE 9

Prison meeting room. The opening scene of the play resumes.

MORRISON
Gunther's up before the Police Board soon. Big fundraiser comin' up for him. I've half a mind to go, see him in action. See Breen too -- he's the master of ceremonies. Maybe he'll say something useful. Maybe Buckley'll be there. I can size her up.

OTHA JEFFRIES
She'll be there, standin' up for her boys. She was part of it. She had to hear me screamin'.

Pause.

MORRISON
Lawyer in my office, former prosecutor, worked with Breen years ago, they used to go to the same church. Says that Breen and his wife ran the parish clothing drive for years, collected old coats for the homeless every winter.

Pause. No response from OTHA.

"Danny Breen," he says, "Great guy."

SCENE 10

December, 1997. ANN BREEN and her sister PEG have baked cookies and are about to frost them. PEG is visiting from California and should be subtly clad to indicate she isn't part of this neighborhood anymore.

ANN
Anyway, he should be home soon. It's been tough on the

ANN *(continued)*
kids. Eileen, all last year, she's staying at home, afraid to
even go to prom. Black kids all thought her dad was a
torturer, and you know at that age, some of the white kids,
they're wanna-bes, go around with their pants around their
knees.

PEG
I sort of figured that. She said something--

ANN
So now she's out by you, she's got a fresh start. Nobody's
heard of Jack Gunther or anybody else. She comes home for
a visit, she just sleeps in, doesn't see anybody.

PEG
And the boys?

ANN
They don't say anything. *(Beat)* Well, once, it came out.
Easter, they were here for dinner, Danny and John got into
an argument. Matt says, "Whad'ya gonna do, Dad? Put a
cattleprod to his balls?" Oh, God. Danny was about this far
*(Indicating about a half inch between her index finger and
thumb)* from beating him to a pulp. And you know they live
on the north side now. Might as well be in Wisconsin for
all we see of 'em. They keep talking about moving to
Arizona.

PEG
They're probably scared their dad might go to jail.

ANN
Not gonna happen. Too long, statute of limitations has
expired. It'd have to be the feds – state's attorney sure as
heck ain't gonna do it – and the feds have bigger fish,
terrorists, mafia guys, aldermen.

PEG *(pointing to the cookies)*
These are cool now.

ANN
Watch the TV, listen to the radio, you'll never hear a word about it. I mean white, black, nobody cares.

PEG
Well, then there's nothing to worry about. If nobody cares, nothing's going to happen. Is that enough frosting or do you want me to lay it on thick?

ANN
I mean who's gonna believe a bunch of killers and gangbangers? And Dan's got over a hundred commendations. And the black guys he worked with, they all think he's great.

PEG
Well, there's a little more to it, isn't there? Once you've seen those photos of Donald Calvin –

ANN
That was all Jack Gunther, Danny's hardly mentioned, and I mean maybe Jack lost his temper. The guy did kill two cops.

PEG
Kill two cops and get a punch in the mouth, okay. Kill two cops and get wired up to a shock machine, burned on a radiator, that seems a little different. And it's not just Donald Calvin. I mean those articles, Danny's mentioned a lot.

ANN
So you've been reading those? Where'd you get them?

PEG
A friend sent them to me.

ANN
Really.

PEG
Yeah. They've got Danny in maybe 20 cases.

ANN
Danny worked midnights, that's when they did all the major arrests. So of course they named him more often.

PEG
Still, I think --

ANN *(again, ANN interrupts)*
And their stories, they're describing different machines, some are claiming suffocation, other guys it's beating with a flashlight. I mean what? They got a cabinet full of machines? Sit around, debate which one they're gonna use? Think the black cops are gonna stand for that? Don't you think the state's attorneys, they're in the station all the time, they hear somebody screaming, they're gonna do what? Pretend they didn't hear it?

PEG
Well, yeah. I could see that.

ANN
Oh come on. You know Danny. You've seen him with the kids. I couldn't tell you half the people he's helped from the parish. I mean would a guy like that beat somebody up to get a confession?

PEG
Forget it. Forget I brought it up. Do you want to put
sprinkles on these or something?

ANN
There's some frosting tubes, second shelf. Draw a
Christmas tree or a star or something. *(Beat)* I mean for
somebody who lives a thousand miles away, you sure seem
to be reading every word.

PEG
Well, yeah. I mean I've still got some friends here. You're
my sister. I'm worried about you. Is that a crime?

ANN
Well it doesn't sound like worry. Sounds like nosy.

PEG
Oh, Christ. How long have I been here? Three hours?

ANN
I'm sorry.

PEG
Look, that reporter called me, okay.

ANN
Called you?

PEG
Got my name from – you remember Mary DeFarco?

ANN
Jeez, I haven't heard, I mean, we called her Mary DeFatso. Is
she still as big as a barn?

PEG
I've no idea. Somehow he knew her, she told him I was
Danny's sister-in-law, he tracked me down, thinking I don't
know what. I told him I hadn't lived here in years, I was out
of it, and I didn't believe any of it.

ANN
Right. These guys were criminals. They confess to
something, realize they shouldn't have, and then they make
up a story.

PEG
Okay. I'm not takin' their side.

ANN
Well it sounds like you believe it.

PEG
Well, don't you find it odd, so many named Danny?

ANN *(suddenly)*
He's here.

*DAN BREEN enters through the back door, dressed for the
cold. This is the first time he's seen PEG in a good while
and he's exuberant in his greeting.*

BREEN
Well if it isn't the black sheep, returned to the frozen
tundra.

PEG
Merry Christmas, Danny.

*They embrace platonically. DAN goes on to kiss his wife. He
talks while taking off his winter gear.*

BREEN
You too. Great to have you. And I suppose this weather
doesn't move you to think fond thoughts of home, eh?

PEG
Actually, this is perfect. Beautiful to look at for a few hours,
then it reminds me why I left in the first place.

BREEN
We'll win you over yet. You'll see. It's in your blood.
Indelible.

PEG
Right. Kind of a combination of an infection and a bad
tattoo.

BREEN
Oh, come on. Confess. Deep down, you love the place.

PEG
Try all you like, Danny, you'll get no confession outta me.

ANN *(admonishing)*
Peg.

BREEN *(with good humor)*
There it is. Do you sharpen that tongue every morning or
does it retain its edge through constant use?

ANN
Okay, both of you, stop it.

BREEN
Where's Stephen?

ANN
Danny, for God's sake, it's Jim. And he's very nice.

PEG
Stephen's history. Jim's in with the TV. The weather
channel, probably. He thinks he's accidentally landed in
Alaska.

BREEN *(taking two beers from the refrigerator)*
I meant to buy him some light beer. Maybe he can stomach
a real one?

Welcome home, Peg.

PEG
Thanks. Good to be here.

BREEN exits.

PEG *(conspiratorially, so Dan doesn't hear)*
So you're not in any way suspicious?

ANN
Peg, you think this is some big deal. I can assure you it isn't.
Nobody cares. Now come on. It's Christmas Eve. No more.

SCENE 11

*December, 1997. MAUREEN BUCKLEY, once a rising star,
has been given a lateral transfer which is actually a
demotion. Her office is now in the basement. DAN BREEN
knocks on the door and enters.*

BREEN
The dedicated prosecutor still at her desk.

BUCKLEY
Hello, Dan. Welcome to my new office. One of your court
days?

BREEN
Yeah. Judge Arkovich. A motion to suppress evidence.

BUCKLEY
Did the good guys win?

BREEN
Oh yeah. Never a problem with Arkovich.

BUCKLEY
So you just decided you'd drop in?

BREEN
Yeah, hadn't seen you in a while, was wonderin' what you're up to.

BUCKLEY
Maybe wonderin' what I'm down to, more like it.

BREEN
Well I heard that you weren't on five any more.

BUCKLEY
Didn't know I was in the basement? Running the high profile consumer affairs department? With a staff of two and a budget of hundreds of dollars?

BREEN
Well it's great that you're a department head.

BUCKLEY
Great. Fantastic. Everyone dreams of working down here. Anyway, how're you?

BREEN
Good. Got a great bunch of guys in narcotics now. We're havin' a blast.

BUCKLEY
And Ann and the kids?

BREEN
Daughter's doin' good. She's in school out in California.
Sons are on the north side, of all places. God, they get big
fast. And how's your dad?

BUCKLEY
He's back on his feet, pulling pints as we speak, good as
new. Thanks for asking. And thanks for sending Bill O'Shea
to him. He's had about five retirement parties since, and
last summer, O'Shea's son started bringing his softball team
in. Wednesday nights, the place was full of cops.

BREEN
That's great. You comin' to Gunther's fundraiser?

BUCKLEY
Much as I'd like to see you in action, I can't.

BREEN
It'll be a big crowd, lotta people you know. Your boss is
comin'.

BUCKLEY
We're not seein' eye to eye at the moment.

BREEN
Oh. Sorry to hear that.

BUCKLEY
These things happen.
Beat.

BREEN
Hey, has Bob Moretti talked to you?

BUCKLEY
Dan, nobody talks to me. What's this about?

BREEN
It's the Otha Jeffries case.

BUCKLEY
Jeffries.

BREEN
1986, the kid with the big mouth, set that fire.

BUCKLEY
Danny, I know who you mean. One of those little cases that grows as it gets older.

BREEN
Well, this guy got his reopened. Don't ask me how. I haven't seen the decision. It's not a new trial yet, it's just a hearing.

BUCKLEY
And let me guess – the issue at hand is whether the confession was voluntary?

BREEN
Yeah.

BUCKLEY
So? You'll take the stand, say you never touched him. Your word against his. The office hasn't lost one of those yet.

BREEN
No.

BUCKLEY
He doesn't have any medical evidence, does he?

BREEN
No. *(Beat)* It's just that there's some talk about where you might be on all this.

BUCKLEY
Ahh.

BREEN
Moretti's worried that maybe Jeffries' attorney will call you as a witness. So it's better if we do.

BUCKLEY
Well, Dan, the problem is I still have one or two friends left upstairs, and they tell me it's not as open and shut as you seem to think. I don't know if there's another suspect, if they think somebody else did it, or what, but there's a little concern up there that maybe they didn't tell you about. So maybe you guys meant well –

BREEN
"You guys" meant well? Like you and everybody else wasn't part of it? I can't believe what I'm hearin' here, Maureen. I half expect it from those idiots on the Police Board, people wantin' Jack to pay for doin' what the city wanted. But I never thought I'd hear it from you.

BUCKLEY
Well, that's one way to look at it, Danny, but --

BREEN
We didn't decide to prosecute 'em. We didn't ask for the death penalty. That was you guys. We didn't sentence them to die – a bunch of fuckin' judges did, a lot of them used to work right here, guys we know who took confessions with us. Supreme Court's upheld every one of these convictions. So don't give me this "you guys" stuff. You want to change sides, fine, just keep in mind, Maureen, that you're talkin'

BREEN *(continued)*
about bringin' the whole house down, and it's full of a
whole lotta people, not just a few cops who've been your
friends for years.

BUCKLEY
You think you're tellin' me somethin' I don't know? You
think I want to see my friends in the dock? Why do you
think I'm down here? I didn't testify, didn't make a phone
call, never talked to the press, didn't do a thing but ask one
question too many. So don't think I haven't thought about
this. You tell me how I get on the stand, swear to tell the
truth, and not sit down with blood on my hands.

BREEN
Blood on your hands? Christ, these guys get back on the
street you'll be in blood up to your eyeballs. And you'd be
responsible. Try livin' with that. Otha Jeffries gets out, you
think he's gonna clock in every day, ride the train to the
office?

*Beat. BUCKLEY is not going to lose her temper. She's not
going to concede anything, either, but she needs to get
Dawson's name from BREEN.*

BUCKLEY
Maybe not. But I'm not sure that's the question here. Do
you remember that night?

BREEN
Yeah.

BUCKLEY
You came to tell me the interrogation was finished, I was on
the fire escape?

BREEN
Oh, yeah. The old building. Everybody used to go out there
for a smoke.

BUCKLEY
Do you remember who I was out there with?

BREEN
You were out there with somebody?

BUCKLEY
Yeah, a black detective.

BREEN
I don't think we had any blacks on midnights.

BUCKLEY
He worked afternoons. Older guy, heavy-set, I have the
feeling he wasn't Jack's favorite.

BREEN
Christ, I got no idea who you're talkin' about. *(Beat)* George
Dawson, maybe? Had a drinking problem. Jack busted him
down to patrolman.

BUCKLEY
You happen to know where he is?

BREEN
I haven't heard anything about him in years. Christ, I bet
he's dead, way things were goin'. I think he's got a son on
the job now.

BUCKLEY
Well....okay.

Pause.

BREEN
So what am I gonna tell them upstairs?

BUCKLEY
Oh, I don't know. Maybe just tell 'em we talked and we're still friends. Let them read whatever they want into that.

BREEN
Okay.

BREEN starts to exit.

BUCKLEY
Hey.

BREEN
Yeah.

BUCKLEY
Happy New Year.

BREEN
Oh yeah. Same to you. *(Pause)* Sorry you're down here.

SCENE 12

January, 1998. The action on the stage alternates. MORRISON continues questioning OTHA while BREEN addresses a rally in a Teamsters Union hall filled with supporters of Area 2 Commander Jack Gunther, the audience functioning as that crowd.

MORRISON
Otha, the ground may be shifting here. Gunther's up before

MORRISON *(continued)*
the Police Board. It may be 25 years late, but he's there.
You got a hearing, which is more than most guys got. And
you've got me. But if you wanna keep me, you gotta tell me
what they did to you.

*OTHA does not respond. After a pause, the lawyer
resumes.*

MORRISON
Your son. He's 12 now? You'll see him five, six more
times, then you're dead. You want him to watch you die?

BREEN
Good evening and thanks for coming. As most of you
know, Jack Gunther, who is standing over there in all his
glory, can't take the microphone tonight thanks to his
lawyer, who has imposed a gag order on him. The only good
part of that is that I can say whatever I want to about him,
knowing that for once, he can't contradict anything I say.

MORRISON
So what does the basement look like?

OTHA JEFFRIES
It's dark. *(Remembering)* Old refrigerator, really old, had
one of those handles you gotta pull down to open. Name
across the front, starts with a P. That's the first thing you
see at the bottom of the stairs. Turn right, there's some
rusty old lockers.

BREEN
I first met him twenty-five years ago, in 1973. I come in one
day and here's this new sergeant, young guy, just a few
years older'n me, we're both Vietnam vets. I went up,
introduced myself, he shook my hand, I'm thinking, "Nice
fella," and he says, "Nice to meet you, Dan. Get a haircut."

MORRISON
What happened after Gunther pushed you down those last
two steps?

OTHA JEFFRIES
They handcuffed me to a pipe that comes hanging out of the
ceiling. I was like this, hanging.

MORRISON
What specifically did each one do?

OTHA JEFFRIES
Breen handcuffs my ankles to some little pole they got on
the floor. DeLuca pulled my pants down, then my shorts.
Gunther takes this cloth that was hanging over the pipe,
shoves it in my mouth. Fuckin' dirty, smelled real bad.

BREEN
Back in '77, we get a call of a gunshot in a six flat, 68th and
Langley. Jack decides to go along for the ride. We get there,
this older black guy's bleeding all over the linoleum, shot in
the arm. This teenager's pointin' a gun at him. Woman's
unconscious on the floor, her nose smashed up, blood all
over her bathrobe. The kid has this blank, dazed look, he's
shakin', and I'm ready to pop him, my partner's the same,
and Jack pushes right past us, hasn't got his gun out, both
his hands in the air, talkin', not yellin', to the kid, who
suddenly seems to realize there's somebody else there. And
for a second he points the gun at Jack, and I'm movin' for a
clean shot when I realize -- he's handing Jack the gun.
Turns out this isn't a home invasion, it's a domestic. The
kid's been beaten by his father for 15 years, has the scars to
prove it – cigarette burns, welts, you name it -- and that
night, the father decked the mother and the kid just
snapped. Today, that kid is a Chicago fireman, savin' lives
every day, thanks to Jack.

OTHA JEFFRIES
Then Breen opened this little black suitcase. Inside was
somethin' that looked like a curling iron, had a cord comin'
out of it. Breen plugged it in...

MORRISON
And what did he do with it?

OTHA JEFFRIES
Placed it under my balls. Tried to holler but I couldn't make
any noise. I was cryin', beggin' them to stop. But they
wouldn't take the cloth outta my mouth, so it was like I was
chokin'. Did that three times. Stopped. Then Breen said,
"I don't think he's ready yet." So he touched it to the crack
of my rectum. I'm screamin', top of my lungs, but I got no
sound. Then Gunther, he took the cloth out of my mouth
and I said, "I'll say anything you want. Just stop."

BREEN
Now this is the same guy who's allegedly a detriment to the
force. This is the same guy, certain people are callin' a
torturer. And you all know how this is all based on the
complaints of Donald Calvin, cop killer, thief, con man,
gangbanger, a man who has lied since the day he was born.
It was Jack Gunther who tracked him down -- led the raid,
never afraid to put his life on the line.

OTHA JEFFRIES
After that Breen and DeLuca took me back to the room
upstairs, told me what they wanted me to say to the state's
attorney. And I don't know why I said it, but I said I wasn't
going to say shit to anyone cuz I didn't do nothin'.

BREEN
Jack Gunther is a war hero with three Bronze stars and a
Purple Heart, the best policeman I have ever known, a man
who has dedicated his life to this city. But Donald Calvin's

BREEN *(continued)*
word is apparently more important than Jack's. Donald
Calvin and his fellow travelers, they're the terrorists of the
south side. 'Cept they're worse. Terrorists got some
religion. These guys, their religion is drugs, rape, robbery,
murder.

OTHA JEFFRIES
Breen comes back a couple minutes later. I can tell he's up
to somethin', but I don't know what. Says to DeLuca and
Gunther, "State's attorney's here." Then Gunther must
have flipped the light switch cause everything went dark and
then this plastic bag was over my face.

BREEN
I mean do you see their neighborhoods risin' up against us,
callin' us torturers?

OTHA JEFFRIES *(simultaneously with BREEN)*
No!

BREEN
No, and I'll tell you why. They want safe streets too. And
that's what we tried to give 'em, what Jack fought to give
'em.

OTHA JEFFRIES
Couldn't breathe. Tried to bite it, put a hole in it, but I
couldn't. It was thick.

BREEN
Look at our clearance rates. Christ, we were in the high 90s,
twice we hit a hundred percent. Me, Jack, the other guys,
we'd have been ashamed to post anything less.

OTHA JEFFRIES
I couldn't get any air.

BREEN
We'd have been lettin' down the community. The black community.

OTHA JEFFRIES
Took it off. I'm screamin'. I thought, "I'm gonna die."

BREEN
We were their front line, we were all they had, and we gave it everything we had.

OTHA JEFFRIES
And I hollered, "Whatever you want! I'll say whatever you want!"

BREEN
And Jack Gunther gave most of all. When the history books are written, he will go down as a true American hero. God bless Jack, God bless you, and God bless the city of Chicago.

End of ACT 1.

ACT 2
SCENE 1

Spring, 1998. ALBERT and RITA JEFFRIES enter a private visiting room with MORRISON at the prison where OTHA JEFFRIES is held. RITA thanks the guard who has let them in.

RITA JEFFRIES
Thank you, Officer.

MORRISON
It's usually just a few minutes till they bring him in. I'll just have a quick word with the supervisor, be back when Otha gets here.

MORRISON leaves.

ALBERT JEFFRIES
Not lookin' forward to this.

RITA JEFFRIES
I know.

ALBERT JEFFRIES
Seemed like a good idea when he *(indicating MORRISON)* suggested it, but now....

RITA JEFFRIES
Yeah.

ALBERT JEFFRIES
I could leave.

RITA JEFFRIES
No. That'd just make it worse.

ALBERT JEFFRIES
Does Otha know Gunther got fired?

RITA JEFFRIES
This isn't Siberia, Albert. They do get news.

ALBERT JEFFRIES
So does that put him in a good mood?

RITA JEFFRIES
What do you think? Man on death row, think that's gonna
change him into Mr. Sunshine?

Pause.

ALBERT JEFFRIES
Wish Theo was here. Break the ice.

RITA JEFFRIES
You know he don't like comin' here.

ALBERT JEFFRIES
Got somethin' to tell everybody. Thought it'd be good for
him to hear it too.

RITA JEFFRIES
George Dawson said somethin'?

ALBERT JEFFRIES
No. I think he's probably ashamed. Some of these guys in
here are gonna die cause he said nothin', and he's gonna
come clean? Lose every friend he ever had. His sons, that'd
be the end for them. End of his job too.

But even if we don't get him, I got somethin' else.

RITA JEFFRIES
Oh yeah?

ALBERT JEFFRIES
I've got a contribution for the Free Otha campaign.

RITA JEFFRIES
After all these years you were gonna try to buy him off?

ALBERT JEFFRIES
I'm contributing information.

RITA JEFFRIES
Lord Jesus, I should have known. That wallet sealed in concrete.

ALBERT JEFFRIES
This is better than money.

RITA JEFFRIES
Oh yeah?

ALBERT JEFFRIES
Yeah.

ALBERT wants to wait until after OTHA arrives to reveal his information so he says nothing more.

RITA JEFFRIES
Well?

ALBERT does not respond.

Albert, stop playin' games. Tell me.

ALBERT JEFFRIES *(hesitates, then reluctantly speaks)*
A crackhead, Robert Simpson, sometimes slept in the
garage across from that house where those people got
killed. He was questioned, but they let him go when they
found the car with Otha's prints.

RITA JEFFRIES
He saw somethin'?

ALBERT JEFFRIES
He got convicted in Rockford last year. Set fire to a three
flat. And now they're looking at him for six more fires
around here. All within a half mile of the drug dealer, some
before and some after Otha was arrested.

RITA JEFFRIES
Holy God in heaven.

*ALBERT pulls some paperwork from his jacket, laying it on
the table.*

ALBERT JEFFRIES
My donation.

RITA starts reading the papers.

RITA JEFFRIES
Where'd you get this?

ALBERT JEFFRIES
Guy I worked with years ago, a Polack I always thought was
a racist. Turns out he's the real police.

RITA JEFFRIES
When did you get it? Don't lie to me -- you've had this for a
while.

ALBERT JEFFRIES
Now you wait. After all these years, just for one minute, put yourself in my shoes. One minute. I help Otha, he gets out, he's gonna make my life hell again until he gets arrested for something else, which you know he will. And it took me years to pay the lawyer when he shot that other gangster. Now I'm not payin' for no lawyer again, but I know you, and you will. So where do that leave you and Theo? Also, Otha back on the street, I might never make lieutenant. And what about my girls? They go to cosmetology school? Work in a nail shop? Or here's the other way. I don't help Otha – I make my rank, my girls go to college, and Otha dies. Either way, he makes my life miserable. Either way, I hate myself. So don't you be tellin' me I've had this for a while. But I thought it through and here it is.

OTHA JEFFRIES *(offstage)*
Goddamn spy. You're no guard. You work for the mayor. I bet you're fuckin' related.

Sound of keys in the lock. The door opens and OTHA and MORRISON enter.

He your cousin? Huh? I bet he's your cousin, fuckin' name like that.

MORRISON
Calm down, Otha,

OTHA JEFFRIES *(to the guard)*
Son of a bitch. Lookin' at me, like that. Stop lookin' at me! Why the hell you gotta do that?

MORRISON
Otha, listen--

RITA JEFFRIES
Hello, Otha.

ALBERT JEFFRIES
Hello, son.

OTHA JEFFRIES
Well, well, well. If it ain't my old man. Come to see me after how many years? How many years it been?

ALBERT JEFFRIES
I'm sorry, Otha.

OTHA JEFFRIES
Oh, no problem. I know how hard it is to find a parking space out there. And you probably had to mow the lawn. Go shopping with your lady. Or probably a lot of good TV shows you hadda see.

ALBERT JEFFRIES
Otha, I'm sorry.

MORRISON
The important thing is he's here now, Otha. Now why don't you sit down and we'll--

OTHA JEFFRIES
Motherfucker, I knew you weren't no lawyer. I smelled cop the minute I met you.

MORRISON, RITA, AND ALBERT try to calm OTHA almost simultaneously.

MORRISON
Otha, now, please, let's--

RITA JEFFRIES
Otha, Mr. Morrison is working so hard for you.

ALBERT JEFFRIES
Otha, let's just all sit down and we'll work this out.

OTHA JEFFRIES
I ain't gonna sit down, I'm a busy man, I got appointments, people to see, places to go, you know how it is – right, Dad?

ALBERT JEFFRIES *(to MORRISON)*
I thought you told him.

OTHA JEFFRIES
What?

ALBERT JEFFRIES *(to Rita)*
What's goin' on here?

MORRISON
I didn't think I could get him here if he knew you were coming.

ALBERT JEFFRIES
Otha, I'm sorry. Do you hear me? I'm your father and I'm sayin' I'm sorry.

OTHA JEFFRIES
Oh, you're my father. I was wonderin'. Thought you looked familiar. Well it's very nice to meet you. Now if you'll excuse me, I'll be leavin'. Sound familiar, Dad?

ALBERT JEFFRIES
Otha, now listen. You sit down here, we can work this out. I agree with you, I haven't been much of a father. But I'm tryin' now, tryin' hard as I can, and I can help you. And

ALBERT JEFFRIES *(continued)*
Theo, I do what I can for him, but he needs his father. You gotta see him play ball. He's the spittin' image of you. He can hit, run, throw.

OTHA JEFFRIES *(momentarily not furious)*
Like father, like son.

ALBERT JEFFRIES
Yeah. He's got the temperament too. Like when he's at the plate--

OTHA JEFFRIES *(suddenly infuriated, he interrupts)*
Oh, he's got the temperament, huh? And I don't?

ALBERT JEFFRIES
No, I'm not sayin' ---

OTHA JEFFRIES
That's right, I ain't got the temperament. Let's see you in here, see what kinda fuckin' temperament you got. Fuckin' bitch, come in here after all these years, pretend you're my father.

RITA takes the police reports and hides them out of site. ALBERT attempts to get a word in, but OTHA continues.

ALBERT JEFFRIES
Otha, I didn't mean --

OTHA JEFFRIES
Pretend you motherfuckin' care if I live or die. No, you do care. You'd be a whole lot better off if I was fuckin' dead. I get it. Well thank you very much, but I gotta go.

MORRISON
Otha, hold on a minute.

ALBERT JEFFRIES
Otha, please. I got somethin' to show you. I can help you.

He motions to the table, but the police reports aren't there. He looks at Rita accusingly.

RITA JEFFRIES
Otha, could you please just settle down?

ALBERT JEFFRIES *(to Rita)*
What are you doin'?

RITA JEFFRIES
Albert, haven't you done enough?

ALBERT JEFFRIES
Give it to me.

OTHA JEFFRIES
Leave her alone. I don't want nothin' you got. Guard. Guard. Guard. Yo.

MORRISON
Otha, now come on.

OTHA JEFFRIES
Why the hell you do this to me? Motherfucker!

ALBERT JEFFRIES
Son!

MORRISON
Otha, wait a minute. We're all here for—

ALBERT JEFFRIES
Son, please, don't do this.

The door opens.

OTHA JEFFRIES *(to ALBERT)*
You have a nice day, now. Drive safely. Wouldn't want anybody in this family to get killed.

OTHA goes out as MORRISON keeps pleading, and at the last second, MORRISON goes out the door just as it closes. We hear the sound of the door being locked.

MORRISON
Otha, wait. Listen. Guard, hold on a minute. *(To ALBERT and RITA)* Sorry.

The door closes and locks. Pause.

RITA JEFFRIES
I'm sorry, Albert.

ALBERT JEFFRIES
What the hell are you doin'? Why'd you hide my reports?

RITA JEFFRIES
You think it's all about you. All you can think about's yourself. You show up today, ready to play hero, and it doesn't go according to your plan, and you don't realize that he's like that all the time, comes in yellin' and screamin'. Mother F this and mother F that. Settles down for a little while, then all of a sudden goes off again. He's like a bomb. Albert, he's sick.

ALBERT JEFFRIES
He ain't sick. He's just a loud-mouthed-wise—

RITA JEFFRIES *(interrupting)*
No. Somethin's broken, somethin's snapped. It's gotten worse. Goes on all the time about the FBI, watchin' him on

RITA JEFFRIES *(continued)*
cameras. I gotta watch every word I say or he can blow up,
scare everybody in the room. Families around, little kids,
he don't care what language he uses. I got to apologize to
everybody. Guards, the other families, I can see they hate to
see me there, ruins everybody's visit.

Albert, I don't want him dead. But I don't want him home.

ALBERT JEFFRIES
After all you been doin'?

RITA JEFFRIES
He wasn't crazy all those years -- well he was a little, but it's
getting' worse. Now you come and drop this, *(pulling
evidence back out)* don't give me no time to think about it.
And I gotta think about more than myself. I gotta think
about Theo. I broke my back bringing up that kid, you just
show up for baseball, take him to the movies. I'm not havin'
all I done wrecked. Otha comes home, he gonna wanna live
with you? What's he gonna do, a man in that condition,
other than steal and sell drugs? You give the man that file,
you the hero. You wreck Theo's life, you wreck my life, but
you feel good.

ALBERT JEFFRIES
Now hold on a minute. I –

RITA JEFFRIES
Look, it's out there, the police have it. Let God do it. If he
brings Otha back to me, okay, I'll carry that burden. But I'm
not gonna let you wreck two more lives on the spur of the
moment just so you can bask in glory.

ALBERT JEFFRIES
I can't believe you'd sit on this.

RITA JEFFRIES
You did.

ALBERT JEFFRIES
You're scared of him.

RITA JEFFRIES
You aren't? You think that was all a show?

ALBERT JEFFRIES
What's the worst that could happen?

RITA JEFFRIES
Gets out, kills somebody. Kills hisself.

ALBERT JEFFRIES *(pauses as this sinks in)*
Kills me? Kills you?

RITA JEFFRIES
Who do he hate worst of all?

ALBERT JEFFRIES
Oh Jesus.

RITA JEFFRIES
Breen. Gunther. The Mayor.

ALBERT JEFFRIES
Safer for everybody, he stays inside? *(Beat)* So what do we do?

He motions to the paperwork on the table, as if to say, "Do we hand this over or not?" Long pause.

ALBERT JEFFRIES
No, we gotta give it to the lawyer. Can't play God. That's what they did.

Sound of door unlocking.

RITA JEFFRIES
Put that away. Don't you say a word.

RITA and ALBERT exit.

SCENE 2

MORRISON and OTHA enter OTHA's cell, immediately following previous scene.

OTHA JEFFRIES
I want Leslie back.

MORRISON
Otha, listen.

OTHA JEFFRIES
Got some more surprises for me? You wanna bring Gunther in here?

MORRISON
Otha, you know—

OTHA JEFFRIES *(interrupting)*
Maybe Breen's runnin' a little late?

MORRISON
Otha, shut the fuck up! *(Pause)* You may hate him, but your dad is trying to help.

OTHA JEFFRIES
You don't know shit about my dad.

MORRISON
Maybe. But you don't know shit about how to get out of

MORRISON *(continued)*
this place.

OTHA JEFFRIES
And you do, motherfucker?

MORRISON
A helluva lot more than you! But you gotta decide. You
want to die, that's just fine, your call, but I ain't gonna tag
along for that ride -- I'm out. I'm done today. You can shit
on everyone who's trying to help you – your dad, your mom,
me – or you can shut the fuck up, and accept the fact that
we're all you've got. *(Pause)* You decide.

Pause.

Decide, Otha.

Pause.

Alright, I'm out.

MORRISON starts to leave.

OTHA JEFFRIES
Hold up.

MORRISON stops and just stares at OTHA. Long pause.

Okay.

MORRISON
Okay what?

OTHA JEFFRIES
Okay, motherfucker, I'll do what you goddamn want.

SCENE 3

Early September, 1998. Late evening in the Breens' house in Chicago. ANN and PEG are drinking wine while they clean up the kitchen. They are dressed as if for a funeral. PEG is sober. ANN is not. There's a wine bottle on the table or countertop that's partly full, and during this conversation, ANN keeps pouring more into her glass.

ANN
I think maybe the potato salad was a little too salty.

PEG
It was fine. Everything was perfect and your eulogy was beautiful. Aunt Dorothy would have been proud.

ANN
The desserts went down well.

PEG
Christ, Sheila was so excited I think she forgot her mother was dead.

ANN
Well you really put your foot in it tonight.

PEG
What?

ANN
You said you were shocked about four times.

PEG
Oh, Christ, it's just a figure of speech.

ANN
Jesus, how could you do that?

PEG
Oh, give me a break. Like Danny's some sensitive guy.

ANN
He hasn't been through enough without you adding to it?

PEG
Been through? What's Danny been through?

ANN
Well you know he didn't want to leave the police. Couple months ago, a guy from the mayor's office took him aside, because of all those articles, said it was time to go and they could get him a job with the sheriff.

PEG
So that's what Danny's been through? He gets another good job, now he's gonna get two pensions, and that's makin' him suffer? Give me a fucking break! I mean do you ever think about what Danny did?

ANN
He didn't do anything. You gotta be outta your mind. Jack Gunther, maybe. Rudy DeLuca, maybe. But not Danny.

PEG
So you've got an interrogation room, one prisoner, Dan and Gunther. And what? Old Jack pulls down the guy's pants, takes out the machine, shocks the guy, asks the questions, zips the guy up, and Danny's just standin' there?

ANN
You just don't have a clue. You sit all high and mighty, no kids, a new man every five years, and pass judgment on us hicks you left behind. You haven't got any idea what it's like. You weren't here when Donald Calvin killed those two cops.

PEG
Well I'm sorry for those cops – and their families, but I got news for you. Look at the dates. Danny and Gunther were doing this for years before those two were shot. And as for me, you got it right. I don't live here. Thank God. And I don't have kids. And you're right, it's the new man every few years. It's the sight of a different dick, keeps your mind nimble. Ask Danny. He seems to have liked the view too.

ANN
Well, fuck you.

PEG
Well this is a day to remember. I don't think I've ever heard you say fuck before.

ANN
Fuck you. You just hate Dan.

PEG
Hate Dan? No, actually I like him quite a bit. Hate what he did, but I can't help it, I like him. And I know a lot of those guys were guilty--

ANN *(interrupting)*
Oh, so it doesn't matter what happens to the guilty ones?

PEG
That's not what I'm sayin'. I'm sayin' it's not okay for anybody, 'cause how can you be sure somebody's guilty? And it looks like Danny and his pals got some guys who were innocent.

ANN
According to who? You and your California friends?

PEG
You are absolutely fucking blind.

ANN
I'm fucking blind?

PEG
Open your eyes. No, you don't even have to do that, a blind man could see this. Count up the guys he tortured, count up the perjury, and I'll bet you dollars to donuts that Danny committed more crimes than anybody he put away.

ANN
Don't. Please. Let's just stop, okay. Please. I hate fighting with you. I hate it more than anything. I'm going to be sick tonight. I won't sleep. I'll replay this and I'll hate you, then I'll hate me, then I'll hate Danny. Please, Peg. Can we get past this?

PEG
Get past this? I didn't bring it up. I had no intention of talking about it. Christ, you started it and-

ANN *(shouting)*
Okay! *(Pause)* It's just that out of all the relatives, you're about the only one Danny really likes. *(Pause)* He says you're Chicago on the inside.

PEG
Oh, God. I hope not.

ANN
Anyway. *(Beat)* I'm sorry about the no kids. I'm really sorry. I shouldn't have said that.

PEG
Yeah. Okay. Forget it.

ANN
Sorry about the man thing too.

PEG
Yeah.

Long silence. PEG is still wounded, but ANN is hopeful that the argument is over.

Let me ask you something.

Pause, as if she is considering whether to do this or not.

Do you remember when Aunt Dorothy shut down the beauty parlor, we were all over there clearing it out?

ANN
Yeah?

PEG
Do you remember a little black suitcase we pulled out? We opened it up, there was a thing inside, looked like a curling iron, with all these different attachments?

ANN
No.

PEG
I'd seen it before. I was in there one Saturday helping her and she pulled it out and used it on a wart on some old lady's hand.

ANN
She removed warts? Jesus, what she got into.

PEG
It heated things underneath the skin. It was supposed to

PEG *(continued)*
cure anything. Got banned in the 50s, but you can still buy
them on S&M websites. Used to be called a violet ray
machine, now they call it a "shock wand." Advertise it as
causing sharp, painful shocks. Turns out that thousands
were manufactured in Chicago.

ANN is listening but silent.

You don't get it? For God's sake, this is the mysterious
device. This is what Dan and his pals used on those guys.
About five of them said Dan had something that you plug
into the wall, looked like a curling iron, and that's exactly
what it looks like.

ANN *(challenging)*
So?

PEG
So these south side gang guys, go to the worst schools in
the country, are describing an extinct device, they don't
know what it is, nobody knows what it is, Gunther's million
dollar lawyer says it doesn't exist. But it does, and these
guys have described it. Doesn't that increase their credibility
about a hundred percent?

ANN
Well, I don't know. Maybe they all read about it somewhere.

PEG
They don't fucking read! If they did, they'd know the name
of it. None of them does.

Long pause here as ANN thinks this over.

ANN
So when did you figure this out?

PEG
I don't know. When did she fall the first time? You called
about her, I'd talked to the reporter. Somehow the two of
them together got me to wondering. So I did some
research.

ANN
So you've known for maybe a year and a half?

PEG
Yeah.

ANN
And you haven't told anybody?

PEG
Only you.

Another pause as ANN puts this together.

ANN
So Danny's right. You do have Chicago inside.

PEG
What?

ANN
You didn't tell that reporter, you didn't tell anybody. How's
that different from Danny? He's protecting Jack and Rudy
and the others. He knows they're basically good, the other
guys are basically evil. I mean maybe he was in the room
when something happened, maybe he wasn't. But you're
sort of in the room too. You know this secret, and it's not
like you're interested in seeing these guys out of prison or
you would've told somebody.

PEG
I'm in the room. Christ.

ANN
You're the greatest. I feel a whole lot better.

PEG
You know I –

ANN *(interrupting)*
Danny's always been right about you. You can take the girl
out of Chicago, he says, but you can't take Chicago out of
the girl.

PEG
But...

ANN
I think I'll go to bed. All this wine. You know I have one
glass at night, Danny says it makes me mean. But I just like
it. Haven't had this much in a while, though. Anyway, Mass
in the morning. I'd skip it, but Danny's gotta usher. But
you sleep in. We'll have a nice breakfast, and then we'll get
you to the airport.

PEG
Okay.

ANN
I'm sorry for the things I said. Are we okay?

PEG
We're okay. Good night.

ANN
I just don't want to be alone, you know.

PEG
Yeah.

SCENE 4

November, 1998. At the auto pound, BREEN walks in on DAWSON. In the original production, a buzzer sounded as if someone was being buzzed in through a security door each time one of the subsequent visitors arrived, and the audience could see a figure enter a trailer on one of the security cameras overhead. This helped convey to the audience that all of the visitors are not there are the same time, but that is how the visits seem to DAWSON.

BREEN
George, how ya doin'?

DAWSON
Hello.

BREEN
Long time. You're lookin' well.

DAWSON
Yeah. You too.

BREEN
Man, you gotta great set-up here. It's so quiet.

DAWSON
Yeah. So what brings you down here?

BREEN
I heard you were here, was in the neighborhood, thought I'd stop by.

BREEN pulls out a pint of whiskey in a brown paper bag and sets it on the table or counter.

DAWSON
A social call. Now why do I have a hard time believin' that?

BREEN
Well, there is somethin' I wanted to talk to you about. But I really was right nearby, so....

DAWSON *(waiting, not making it easy for BREEN)*
Yeah?

MORRISON enters. He hands DAWSON a business card.

MORRISON
Officer Dawson, my name is Robert Morrison. I represent a man named Otha Jeffries, I believe you know his father.

BREEN
Well he's got a hearing comin' up.

MORRISON
I just wanted to ask you a few questions about the night he was arrested.

ALBERT JEFFRIES enters. He holds police reports.

ALBERT JEFFRIES
George. I gotta talk to you about something I found.

MORRISON
You're going to have to testify under oath.

DAWSON
Wasn't my case. I'm not in any of the paperwork.

BREEN
Doesn't matter. Otha Jeffries picked your photo, the state's attorney picked out the same one. So you can do what you want, it's a free country, but you're gonna get subpoenaed just like I am.

BUCKLEY
Officer Dawson. You may not remember me,

BREEN
I came by to see what you remember.

DAWSON
I don't remember anything.

BUCKLEY
When you're sworn in you're going to have to say something, and if you know what that is, I'd be grateful to hear it.

MORRISON
Can you describe his appearance at the various times you saw him?

BREEN
Jack and I remembered that we talked to the kid, didn't get shit, so we sent you in, do the good cop, and it musta worked because he gave it all up afterwards.

DAWSON
That's not how I remember it.

BREEN
Well, maybe you could refresh our memory.

DAWSON
You know, I think I'll just take my time, think about it

DAWSON *(continued)*
some. When I'm called, I'll have it all worked out.

ALBERT JEFFRIES
They charge this other guy now, what does that say about
the confessions of all the other guys?

BREEN
Okay, fair enough.

BUCKLEY
That night, what you said, what I saw, I've tried to forget it,
but I can't.

BREEN
I know you and Jack had your differences. I don't think Jack
handled it very well. I told him, I said, "Hey, George is a
good cop. Anybody who is asking for homicides is a guy
who wants to work."

DAWSON
Oh you did?

ALBERT JEFFRIES
Wasn't your fault, George. Anybody woulda done the same
thing.

DAWSON
You don't know what it was like.

MORRISON
You wanna argue that he's nobody you'd want livin' next
door, okay, fine. But --

BREEN
Jesus, do you remember the mouth on that kid?

DAWSON
He had a mouth all right. Only thing is, I don't think he killed anybody.

BREEN
Oh, come on George. His fingerprints were in the fuckin' car.

DAWSON
Yeah, I know all that. But there was another guy you let go, set a hell of a lot of fires.

ALBERT JEFFRIES
George, I need you.

BREEN
You wanta see Otha Jeffries back on the street? You gonna be responsible for what he does when he gets there? Cause you know it'll be six months, tops, before he's racked up a new set of victims.

MORRISON
You won't be up there alone, George.

BUCKLEY
I'm gonna have to testify.

MORRISON
She been down here to see you?

DAWSON
No.

BREEN
Really? She's an old friend. I thought for sure she was comin'.

DAWSON
Maybe she came on my day off.

BREEN
She'll get sworn in, say there was no sign of injury when she
took his statement.

DAWSON
Probably.

MORRISON
You know she was demoted. Rumor is she started to
question some of those midnight shift confessions.

BUCKLEY
So you won't say? You can't say? *(Beat)* Maybe you've
already said it in some anonymous letters?

DAWSON
Do you have any idea of what's at stake here?

BREEN
He hasn't got a chance in hell.

BUCKLEY
Believe me, I can't stop thinking about it.

MORRISON
We're talking about a man's life here.

ALBERT JEFFRIES
Think of your sons, George. I'd do it for them.

BREEN
We did the right thing. You did the right thing.

DAWSON
Yeah, I hear ya. Listen, I gotta get back to work.

Each character makes for the exit after delivering his or her final lines below.

MORRISON
I gotta get back myself. Thanks for your time, detective.

BREEN
I can ever do anything for you, just let me know.

ALBERT JEFFRIES
They're going through old police reports, looking for the words that were misspelled in the anonymous letters, tryin' to figure out who wrote 'em. You know they're not gonna start with the white guys.

DAWSON
Thanks for the heads up, Albert.

BUCKLEY
See you at the hearing. You want to talk in the meantime, call me. Please.

DAWSON
Yeah.

BREEN has returned and surprises DAWSON.

BREEN
And I hope things continue to go well for your sons.

BREEN leaves. DAWSON contemplates the threat implied in BREEN'S last words.

SCENE 5

November 1998. MORRISON sits waiting for OTHA at the prison. OTHA enters, and for once is not verbally abusing the guard who has escorted him.

OTHA JEFFRIES
Thank you, sir. I appreciate the escort. Lot of dangerous guys around here.

MORRISON looks at him quizzically, wondering why he hasn't heard profanity.

OTHA JEFFRIES
I'm tryin' to confuse 'em.

MORRISON
Is it working?

OTHA JEFFRIES
Might be. That guy actually looked a little scared.

MORRISON
Listen, I got good news. I think Dawson's gonna go our way.

OTHA JEFFRIES
Bullshit.

MORRISON
I think you just might be wrong. And if he does the right thing here, Buckley'll be thinking twice, afraid of perjury, afraid of losing her law license.

OTHA JEFFRIES
Bushman, what in God's name makes you think Dawson's ever gonna say a single thing to help us?

MORRISON
I went to see him. I didn't get much, but I saw cracks, saw that this all was wearing on him. And your dad's been diggin' around too.

OTHA JEFFRIES
My dad couldn't get shit from a toilet.

MORRISON
You're wrong. About a week after your dad went down there, Dawson calls him, outta the blue. Says that he's been thinking about it and he remembers seeing guys get taken down to the basement. He's only been there a couple times when the furnace was actin' up, but your Dad asked him what was down there. He said "some old lockers and a Philco refrigerator with a pull down handle."

OTHA doesn't get it.

Philco with a 'P'.

OTHA JEFFRIES
Fuck, I told you that a year ago. What good does that do us?

MORRISON
It corroborates what you've said. It raises your credibility.

OTHA JEFFRIES
What you mean is you finally believe me.

MORRISON
Otha, would I have spent the whole year, putting my ass out there– taking on some powerful people -- if I didn't believe you?

OTHA JEFFRIES
You and everybody else woulda believed me from the get-go
if I was white. I'm in this predicament because I'm black
and I grew up where I grew up.

MORRISON
A lot of people grew up where you grew up, Otha. And not
all of them are sitting where you are. Let's set aside the fact
that you're a thief, a drug dealer, and a gangster. Are you
here because you're black? Yeah. Would people have
believed you if you were white? Let's say yes to that too.
Now where does that get us?

OTHA JEFFRIES
I'm just sayin'...

MORRISON
Nowhere. For the first time, I think maybe we can win this
thing. Dawson doesn't even have to say he saw people
taken to the basement. He describes what's in the
basement, you describe what you saw down there. That
could do it. There's no reason for them to ever take a
suspect to the basement.

OTHA JEFFRIES
Okay, I get it.

MORRISON
And we have your dad to thank.

OTHA JEFFRIES
So after 12 years the punk ass bitch has finally risen to the
occasion.

SCENE 6

December, 1998. BREEN visits BUCKLEY at her father's tavern. He is sitting at a table with a beer when BUCKLEY enters as if she has been called from the pub's basement.

BUCKLEY
Hello, Dan. You're on the wrong side of the city.

BREEN
Yeah. I was up with my sons, thought I'd stop by. Bears on TV later, thought you might be here helpin' out. (*Motioning toward the bar)* How is he?

BUCKLEY
He's fine. The place is either killing him or keeping him alive, depending on your point of view. Can I get you a shot to go with that? Some Powers maybe?

BREEN
No, I'm good with this. Thanks.

BUCKLEY gets herself a beer and sits down with BREEN.

Am I interrupting anything?

BUCKLEY
No, I was in the back cleaning up. Some people do aerobics. I wrestle kegs of beer.

BREEN
Place looks great.

BUCKLEY
Looks better in the dark. You don't want to see it with all the lights on

BREEN
Lotta things are like that.

Brief pause.

BUCKLEY
So how is it working for the sheriff?

BREEN
I like it. I'm still chasin' some of the same guys I was
chasin' twenty years ago, only they got older and moved to
the suburbs.

BUCKLEY
That's great.

BREEN
So I guess you've heard?

BUCKLEY
Yeah. We're up on Thursday. They did call me on that one.

*Pause. BREEN was talking about Dawson, not the date of
the hearing.*

BREEN
Yeah. Judge Edwards. He's your old boss, right?

BUCKLEY
Sort of. A long time ago.

BREEN
So you'll win one for the good guys.

BUCKLEY
You don't know what I'm gonna say.

BREEN
Not much you can say.

BUCKLEY
Maybe not much, but maybe enough.

BREEN
Well I can't imagine what that would be.

Pause. BUCKLEY says nothing.

BREEN
Anyway, it looks like the lineup'll be Jeffries, me, then you'll
be batting cleanup. You probably heard, Jack's moved to
Florida. They're not gonna fly him up. Jeffries wins, Jack'll
testify at the full hearing, but we don't need him for this.

BUCKLEY
What about Officer Dawson?

BREEN
You didn't hear?

BUCKLEY
Hear what?

BREEN
He died.

BUCKLEY
What?

BREEN
Yeah. He was divorced, lived by himself. He was a drinker
in the old days, maybe he went back to it, I don't know. But
Friday night, he ate his gun.

BUCKLEY
Oh, God.

BREEN
Yeah.

BUCKLEY
Oh, shit. Jesus. Did he leave a note?

BREEN
Apparently not. Hate to see anybody die like that. I always
thought he was a good cop.

BUCKLEY
And a dangerous witness.

BREEN
Nah, I don't think so. I ran into him, by coincidence. He
said he didn't remember anything. Course he was on the
sauce back then, so maybe that was it. *(Pause)* Anyway,
Jeffries'll go first, say all kinds of bullshit. They'll rest, they
haven't got anything else, and then me, then you. Moretti'll
show you the confession, the photo taken afterward, no
marks on him, there'll be a few questions from the other
side, and you'll be out of there. Prob'ly ten minutes. Bring a
coffee with ya, it'll prob'ly still be hot when you're done.

BUCKLEY
You ask a lot of your friends, Dan. I can get up there and
play along, just like everybody has for what, 20 years?
Everybody goes home and lives the good life, except of
course Otha Jeffries, who's got a ticket to die for somethin'
I'm not sure he did, a ticket you punched for him, and the
choir boy, who near as I can tell, never shoplifted a candy
bar, and those hundred other guys, and Jeffries' mom, who
came to see me. Christ, I didn't give her the time of day.

BREEN
Oh come on, Maureen, Otha Jeffries is a thug. He shot people, he sold drugs, and he set that fire, no doubt in my mind. He's a stone killer.

BUCKLEY
Shut up. Just shut up. I can't talk about this. I gotta go. You should leave.

BUCKLEY picks up both beer bottles.

BREEN
Alright. I'm going.

BREEN starts to leave, BUCKLEY wipes off the table. BREEN then comes back.

Hey. Bottom line, you and me, we're the same, same stock, same beliefs, same things in here. *(Tapping his heart)* We're family. We take care of each other. And one day, I hope a long time from now, you'll be cryin' at my wake or I'll be cryin' at yours.

BUCKLEY
Just leave.

SCENE 7

December, 1998, the morning of OTHA's hearing. MORRISON comes into the holding cell with civilian clothes for OTHA to wear in the courtroom. OTHA puts them on through the scene, which plays alternately with what is going on in the Breen and Jeffries households.

OTHA JEFFRIES
Shit, where'd you get those? I'm gonna look like –

MORRISON
Otha, we don't have time for this. Judge don't usually allow it, not for a hearing. He tossed us a bone here. Maybe feelin' sorry for us losing Dawson. Just put 'em on and listen up.

OTHA JEFFRIES
Yes, sir.

MORRISON
It's gonna be war out there today.

RITA JEFFRIES' apartment, December 1998. Paraphernalia should indicate there's an adolescent, Otha's son THEO, living in the flat. There's a knock at the door. RITA is almost ready to leave for court.

RITA JEFFRIES
Hello.

ALBERT JEFFRIES
Sorry. I couldn't find a spot and I didn't want to leave it by the hydrant.

He hands RITA his car keys.

It's by the church driveway.

RITA JEFFRIES
Thanks. He should be home around three.

ALBERT JEFFRIES
No problem. Go ahead, I know you like to get there early.

RITA JEFFRIES
I'm wantin' to go and not wantin' to go.

ALBERT pours himself some coffee, then sits at a table, eating a McDonald's breakfast sandwich that he brought with him.

ALBERT JEFFRIES
I know what you mean. Hard to put much faith in that prosecutor. We really needed George, and I actually thought he'd tell the truth. But now...

The BREENS' kitchen, the morning of OTHA's hearing. DAN BREEN enters with the paper as if he's just brought it in from outside. ANN is about to put breakfast on the table.

ANN
Anything in the paper about it?

BREEN
It's just a hearing. Not even that. It's a hearing to see if he gets a hearing. Nobody's gonna cover it. Only people there'll be waitin' for other cases.

ANN
I just don't think she'll do anything to hurt us. You don't do that to somebody who's been your friend for 12 years.

BREEN
Maybe you're right. It'd be political suicide, nobody'd hire her. But she sees things in black and white. Those idiots on the fifth floor moved her to the basement, so she's already taken a hit. I don't know what the hell she's gonna do.

ANN
You can always contradict her testimony.

BREEN
I gotta go first. She goes the wrong way, though, the state's attorney'll ask her why she never said anything 'till now,

BREEN *(continued)*
with a guy gonna die because she kept quiet.

OTHA
What's the point now without Dawson? What hope have we got?

MORRISON
You and Maureen Buckley. That's the ballgame.

RITA JEFFRIES
I been prayin'. And I can't help it, I think, that's a strong woman, she hadda see or hear somethin', and when she sees me there, she's gonna come through. I'm gonna stand up when she comes in, make sure she can't miss me.

ALBERT JEFFRIES
Don't get yourself thrown out.

RITA JEFFRIES
People standin' up all the time. They don't know if you goin' out or movin' your seat cause some smelly guy next to you or what.

ANN
So, we didn't decide. Am I goin'?

BREEN
I don't know.

ANN
I mean, she sees me, you know, like she thinks about what it's gonna do to us.

BREEN
What the hell, I guess it can't hurt. If she's goin' the wrong way, it might give her something to think about. Just say

BREEN *(continued)*
hello afterward no matter what happens.

ANN
Okay. Third floor, right?

BREEN
Yeah. Judge is Edwards.

ANN
What's the guy's name?

BREEN
Otha Jeffries. Nobody you've ever heard of.

ANN
You know, after all this time, you'd think that this'd be no big deal. But I don't know, this feels different, and I'm wakin' up in the mornin' wonderin'...

BREEN
What?

ANN
I don't know what happened, maybe you had your reasons and you think I couldn't understand, but I need to know, because even if it blows over this time,

BREEN
It'll blow over.

ANN
I'll be wonderin' if there's gonna be a next time, and how many next times there might be, and whether the guy I married is the guy I thought he was or if he's somebody else, and if you're gonna be around for the rest of my life.

BREEN
Today's gonna blow over, guaranteed. I can't say if it's gonna happen again. It makes for a good story and guys are gonna use it to try to get out. But I'm still the guy you married. Same guy. *(Beat)* I gotta get movin'.

ALBERT JEFFRIES
I'm just sayin', I think today, you gotta let it go. What's gonna happen, gonna happen.

RITA JEFFRIES
I know.

ANN
I talked to Peg yesterday.

BREEN
So that's where this is comin' from.

ANN
No, she said good luck. She wishes you well.

BREEN
Yeah.

OTHA JEFFRIES
So, bottom line, it's me against her.

MORRISON
Yeah. Well, it's you against Breen. She's the wild card. You gotta be good, he's gotta be bad, she's gotta give us somethin'.

OTHA JEFFRIES
No other way, is there.

MORRISON
No other way. Just tell the story like you told it to me.
Don't let them bait you. We'll see what we get out of her.
She gives us anything at all, either the judge'll give us a full
hearing or we got a shot to get one on appeal. With the
right ruling, we might be able to bring in other guys who've
been tortured, show a pattern. We get that, new ballgame.

ALBERT JEFFRIES
Maybe the lawyer'll think of somethin'. He loses today,
maybe we oughta give him that file.

RITA JEFFRIES
Albert, we been over that.

ALBERT JEFFRIES
Yeah. Okay. Call me.

He hands her his cell phone.

RITA JEFFRIES
I will.

RITA exits. Albert is unsure of what to do with himself.

ANN
Good luck.

BREEN
Thanks.

MORRISON
I don't wanna hear the word fuck, or shit, or goddamn.

OTHA JEFFRIES
Okay. I get it. I'll do my job.

MORRISON
And Otha, you gotta trust me. I'm doin' everything I can to get you outta here.

OTHA JEFFRIES
You better save my life. Save a lot of lives.

MORRISON
Okay.

OTHA JEFFRIES
Hey.

MORRISON
Yeah?

OTHA JEFFRIES
Thanks.

SCENE 8

A Cook County courtroom, December 22, 1998. RITA JEFFRIES and ANN BREEN sit in separate rows in the audience of the courtroom.

MORRISON *(addressing the judge)*
Your Honor, defending Otha Jeffries isn't easy, not because of who he is or what he is accused of, but because of what his case says about all of us. In this hearing, the voices of other men who make the same claims of torture cannot be heard, and you'll hear only from Mr. Jeffries and the state's two witnesses, the prosecutor who took his confession and one of the police officers who extracted it. The state will ask you to do what this whole city has been doing for years – to look the other way. And that's easy to do, because what Otha Jeffries has to say is too horrible to consider – that detectives, sometimes given to heroism, ran amuck;

MORRISON *(continued)*
that their commanders knew and sanctioned it; that state's
attorneys ignored the abuse, the brutality, and the perjury in
order to get convictions; and that there is a torturable class
in this city, a group of people, beyond the pale of our
compassion, to whom anything can be done. *(A brief pause,
as if time has passed, and then he turns back to Otha, who
is on the witness stand)* Otha, I want to take you back to
what you said earlier, when you were talking about what
happened in the basement, when you were handcuffed to
the pole that comes out of the ceiling.

OTHA JEFFRIES
Yeah.

MORRISON
What did you think was going on when they took you down
the stairs?

OTHA JEFFRIES
When they handcuffed me to the pole, I was just scared, just
not believin' this is happenin' to me. And that stinkin'
cloth in my mouth -- my pants, and I'm there, with my –
genitals hanging out.

MORRISON
Did you try to call for help?

OTHA JEFFRIES
I'm tryin' to scream – but I can't make any noise. And the
pain, it's in your head. I mean it's inside your head. You
don't have any thought. The pain is in your body, yeah, but
it's inside your head.

MORRISON
You were completely helpless?

OTHA JEFFRIES
I'm hangin' there -- cryin' like a baby, I'm chokin' on the
cloth, and I can't breathe cause of the stuff runnin' outta my
nose. I –

Pause. He can't go on.

MORRISON
And the suffocation with the plastic was worse?

OTHA JEFFRIES
The pain was worse in the basement, but upstairs was
worse because I thought I was gonna die. The shock
machine, you can't have no thought, but with the plastic,
you got thought, and you know you gonna die if he doesn't
take it off. And they didn't take it off. I thought I was dead.

MORRISON
Okay, Otha. Just one more question. You stole those tires.
Your fingerprints were in the car. You confessed to the
crime. And you didn't even tell the paramedic who
examined you at the jail that you'd been tortured. So why
should we believe you?

OTHA JEFFRIES
Didn't tell the paramedic? I'm comin' in with 25 other guys
and what am I gonna say? "Hey, Mr. White Man who looks
just like the guys who been torturin' me, could you look at
my dick because some cops have just been shockin' me
there? And when you're done, could you look up my
rectum cause they did it there too?" Why should you
fuckin' believe me? I can't tell you any more than what
happened and you got to believe me because it's true.
Because I couldn't make this up. Because I can't sleep
nights. Guards come in to stop me from screamin' in my
sleep, wakin' everybody up. You make me go through all

OTHA JEFFRIES *(continued)*
this and then, goddamn it...My son, I can count on two
hands the number of times I seen him. I'm dying, alone,
sometimes I think my brain is gone and they took it. They
took my life away for four goddamn tires.

MORRISON
Thank you, Otha. No further questions.

SCENE 9

*RITA JEFFRIES'S apartment. ALBERT is up in THEO'S
room. He has the phone, and checks to make sure it's
working. Looking for a way to calm himself, he sits on the
bed and starts singing.*

ALBERT JEFFRIES
People, get ready, there's a train that's comin'. Don't need
no ticket, you just get on board.

SCENE 10

The courtroom. MORRISON questions BREEN.

MORRISON
So you never touched Otha Jeffries?

BREEN
Well I touched him to put the handcuffs on him.

MORRISON
And nothing else.

BREEN
Nothin'. I mean, if I'd done half of what he says, his body'd
show it. But he's got no medical evidence at all. Got a vivid
imagination though, so good he's invented a shock machine

BREEN *(continued)*
nobody's ever seen. He calls me a torturer – but he's the
guy who shot that kid in the leg. Calls it gang discipline.
That's torture.

MORRISON
Detective, you and I both know that his previous crimes are
off limits here, just like other accusations of torture against
certain police officers cannot be raised in this hearing.

BREEN
I stand corrected.

MORRISON
Did you take him to the basement, handcuff him to a pole,
pull his pants down, and shock him in his genital area?

BREEN
For God's sake, I mean come on, I'm gonna pull a guy's
pants down inside a Chicago police station? You're outta
your mind.

MORRISON
Please answer yes or no.

BREEN
No. Counselor, I know you gotta job to do. You gotta put
me on trial when you know in your heart that I'm the better
human being.

MORRISON
Better than who? Better than Otha Jeffries?

BREEN
Absolutely.

MORRISON
So you're happy to play not just detective but judge too?

BREEN
No, counselor, that's not what I'm sayin'. I'm sayin' that I'm the guy you depend on in the middle of the night when your daughter is missing. I'm the guy who goes into those neighborhoods, who fights for the good people there, who tries to give them safe streets, safe schools, a chance at seein' their kids reach the age of 20 without bein' shot by somebody like Otha Jeffries. He lived in your neighborhood, you'd be glad to have him locked up. Counselor, I been doin' this for 30 years. I know my job, what I can do, what I can't do, what's wrong, what's right. And I don't torture anybody. Never have. Never will.

MORRISON
Can you tell me, detective, what's in the basement?

BREEN
I got no idea. Never had any reason to go there. Maybe Otha Jeffries knows cause he knows the janitor, or his dad went down there, or he's got a friend who shoots up down there now that it's vacant, but I've got no idea.

MORRISON
Thank you, Detective.

SCENE 11

The hallway outside the courtroom. RITA JEFFRIES talks to ALBERT on the cell phone he'd lent her earlier. We also see ALBERT on the phone with her.

RITA JEFFRIES
He just finished. He's a good liar. Lotta practice. Whole lotta.

ALBERT JEFFRIES
But how did Otha do?

ANN enters, looks around for her husband.

RITA JEFFRIES
He got angry at the end, but I think he did okay.

BREEN enters.

ANN
Are you okay?

BREEN
Fine. Never better.

ALBERT JEFFRIES
Do you get any sense of which way the judge is leaning?

RITA JEFFRIES
Oh, I don't know Albert. He just sits on the bench up there, like he's God, shows nothin' on his face.

BREEN
I don't think we need to hang around for the rest of this. Let's get some coffee.

BUCKLEY enters and walks toward the courtroom.

ANN
No, I'm gonna stay.

ANN waves at BUCKLEY, BREEN nods or salutes, and RITA gives her a meaningful look.

ALBERT JEFFRIES
Do you think he's got a chance?

RITA JEFFRIES
I got to go. I'll call you later.

SCENE 12

*The courtroom. MORRISON is questioning MAUREEN
BUCKLEY, who is on the witness stand. ANN BREEN and
RITA JEFFRIES are seated, watching the proceeding.*

MORRISON
Now under questioning from Mr. Moretti you said that
while you were standing on that fire escape you heard a
scream. Did you hear any words?

BUCKLEY
I didn't say scream. I said I heard a shout. And no, I didn't
hear any words.

MORRISON
Just one shout?

BUCKLEY
I think so. It was 12 years ago, it's a little hard to recall.

MORRISON
What sort of a shout? A greeting? A curse? A call for help?

BUCKLEY
Just a shout.

MORRISON
And you say you don't know where it came from.

BUCKLEY
That's right.

MORRISON
But it was from inside the building.

BUCKLEY
I think so. But I don't know who was shouting.

BUCKLEY has provided a detail nobody knew – there was shouting.

MORRISON *(encouraged)*
And this black detective, who was there when you arrived but not when you left, what is his name?

BUCKLEY
I didn't recall it, but a couple of months ago I learned that it was George Dawson.

MORRISON
Do you find it odd that George Dawson, the one guy on duty that night who has never been accused of mistreating anyone, and who has never testified in this case before, committed suicide last week?

BUCKLEY
I didn't know him, really, so I wouldn't dare to speculate.

MORRISON
And in that whole time you were in the station, did you see Detective Breen or Detective DeLuca or Commander Gunther carry anything that could have been an electrical device or anything that could have contained one?

BUCKLEY
No.

MORRISON
From the time you came in the station until the time you

MORRISON *(continued)*
left, did you see a black box?

BUCKLEY
No.

MORRISON
Did you see anything with an electrical cord on it?

BUCKLEY
I suppose the coffeemaker must have had one.

MORRISON
Did you see anything that resembled a curling iron?

BUCKLEY
No.

MORRISON
Did you see a plastic bag?

BUCKLEY
No plastic bag.

MORRISON
How about in the garbage cans? Did you see anything lining the garbage cans?

BUCKLEY
No.

MORRISON
One moment, your honor.

MORRISON has hit a wall here. He has no other questions. He walks back to the defense table, where OTHA sits, and

looks over his notes, hoping to find some inspiration.
Finally, he does.

MORRISON
Ms. Buckley, did you see Detective Breen carry anything
into the interrogation room?

MORRISON has stumbled upon the million dollar question,
as BUCKLEY has been drawing a distinction between a
plastic bag and a typewriter cover. BUCKLEY, clearly torn,
hesitates.

MORRISON *(after a pause)*
Ms. Buckley?

BUCKLEY
Yes. I was just thinking back. I think Detective Breen told
me where the coffee was, but he set his cup down before he
went back in the room.

MORRISON
So you are saying Detective Breen had no cup of coffee
when he walked in the room?

BUCKLEY
Yes.

MORRISON
That's not what I asked. Did Detective Breen carry anything
into the interrogation room?

BUCKLEY *(drawing out – she really doesn't want to lie)*
As far as I can recall, remembering that night....he had
nothing in his hands.

MORRISON *(a brief pause while he parses out the answer)*
Okay. *(Pause)* He had nothing in his hands. But did you see

MORRISON (continued)
him take anything at all into that room that night, anything
other than the clothes on his back?

BUCKLEY (very long pause)
No.

SCENE 13

A room adjoining the courtroom, immediately after
Buckley's testimony.

RITA JEFFRIES
How could she lie like that? You expect it from Breen, but a
lawyer, I thought they had to tell the truth.

MORRISON (morose underneath)
I'm sorry, Mrs. Jeffries. I thought we had her. But Otha
was great out there. Let's wait and see what the judge says.

RITA JEFFRIES
You think we still have a chance?

OTHA JEFFRIES
We ain't got shit! Don't lie to her. Tell her we ain't got a
fuckin' thing. I'm dead.

MORRISON
Things look bad now, Otha, but we're not through yet.

OTHA JEFFRIES
Bullshit.

Pause. MORRISON suddenly looks depressed, as if he
recognizes that OTHA has spoken the truth.

RITA JEFFRIES *(she breaks the long silence)*
Otha, your father and I got some information that could
help. There was another suspect in your case, a guy named
Robert Simpson. He got convicted of setting a fire in
Rockford last year and now the police are looking at him for
a bunch of fires down here, some before the ones in your
case, some after, and all in that same neighborhood. Your
father knows one of the officers and he got the paperwork.

Brings out the documents and hands them to MORRISON.

MORRISON
Why didn't I know about this?

RITA JEFFRIES
Albert got it.

OTHA JEFFRIES *(grabs the documents from MORRISON)*
You had this?

MORRISON
Otha, we couldn't have used it here anyway. The only issue
we could raise here was the voluntariness of the confession.

RITA JEFFRIES
That's why we didn't bring it up. We knew we couldn't use
it in this hearing.

OTHA JEFFRIES
So all this time, you got information that could set me free
and you've just been sittin' on it? What? You don't want
me free? Is that it?

RITA JEFFRIES
Of course I do, Otha.

OTHA JEFFRIES
You're afraid I'll take Theo back.

MORRISON
Otha, it doesn't matter when it came.

OTHA JEFFRIES
Whaddya mean? This clears me.

MORRISON
It doesn't clear you. We can argue that he's an established arsonist and all that, but right now, the police have more evidence against you.

OTHA JEFFRIES
So you're saying I got nothing left?

MORRISON
I'm not --

RITA JEFFRIES *(interrupting)*
But it proves he didn't set that fire, he didn't kill no one. It proves they tortured an innocent man.

OTHA JEFFRIES
It proves it huh? You believe me now?

RITA JEFFRIES
I always believed you Otha. I been fighting hard --

OTHA JEFFRIES
Funny way of fighting. You get this information and keep it secret.

RITA JEFFRIES
Mr. Morrison, please help us. Somebody'll listen to this - the newspapers or that reporter. They won't stand for

RITA JEFFRIES *(continued)*
them torturing an innocent man.

OTHA JEFFRIES
You think they'll listen now because I'm innocent? Because
you finally believe me? You think it only matters that they
tortured me if I'm innocent?

RITA JEFFRIES
Of course not. But you are innocent and that makes what
they did even worse.

OTHA JEFFRIES
Well maybe I'm guilty.

MORRISON
I'm going to give you two some privacy.

MORRISON leaves in a hurry.

OTHA JEFFRIES
You ever think of that?

RITA JEFFRIES
Otha, don't.

OTHA JEFFRIES
If I was guilty, would you think I deserved it?

RITA JEFFRIES
Otha, you are innocent.

OTHA JEFFRIES
How do you know? Because your church boy couldn't kill
no one? What if I did kill some fuck who was feedin' drugs
to the mother of my son and I never knew the old people
were in the house?

RITA JEFFRIES
Otha!

OTHA JEFFRIES
So it's all okay, Mrs. Jeffries. He ain't no choir boy. He sells drugs and steals tires and he killed a few people so we just tortured him a little to get him to confess. I'm sure you can see, we did the right thing, gettin' him off the street. That all right by you, Mrs. Jeffries?

RITA JEFFRIES
Otha!

Knock at the door.

MORRISON *(comes in the door)*
The judge is back.

OTHA and MORRISON exit. RITA, stunned, staggers into a chair.

SCENE 14

RITA JEFFRIES' apartment. ALBERT is upstairs in THEO'S room. THEO enters the front door, having returned home from school.

THEO/OTHA JEFFRIES
Anybody home? Grandpa?

ALBERT JEFFRIES
I'm upstairs, Theo.

ALBERT comes down stairs.

THEO/OTHA JEFFRIES
Grandma still gone?

ALBERT JEFFRIES
Yeah. We should be hearing something soon.

THEO/OTHA JEFFRIES
So maybe, I mean there's a chance he could come home?

ALBERT JEFFRIES
Wouldn't happen right away, but if he wins today, he's got a chance.

THEO/OTHA JEFFRIES
Why aren't you there?

ALBERT JEFFRIES
He didn't want me to come. Didn't want me to see this.

THEO/OTHA JEFFRIES
He don't like you.

ALBERT JEFFRIES
Yeah, that too. You know you look just like him. I mean, when he was your age. He had the moves. And talk about quick, my Lord. Brain went about 90 miles an hour. Mine was doin' 30. Those were great days.

THEO/OTHA JEFFRIES
So what happens if he gets out? Grandma says he can't get a job, he can't do anything, and he'll have to live here.

ALBERT JEFFRIES
She may be right. You treat a man like that, maybe he's never gonna be right in the head. Doesn't matter what he did or didn't do.

THEO/OTHA JEFFRIES
But if he comes home, what's gonna happen to me?

ALBERT JEFFRIES
Don't you worry, Theo. I'll be here for you.

THEO/OTHA JEFFRIES
But you don't live here. What if he decides to take me away?

ALBERT JEFFRIES
Oh, don't you worry about that. Okay?

THEO/OTHA JEFFRIES
Yeah.

Pause.

ALBERT JEFFRIES
This waitin' is hard. I'm glad you're with me. *(Beat)* We'll get through this. Might be hard, but we'll be okay.

He looks out the window.

ALBERT JEFFRIES
Looks like it's gonna snow.

Phone rings as the lights come down.

End of play.

JOHN CONROY was born in Chicago and graduated from the University of Illinois in Urbana-Champaign. He was instrumental in exposing the Chicago police torture scandal involving allegations against Commander Jon Burge and others. Over the course of the last three decades, he repeatedly reminded an indifferent public that justice had not been done. Much of his coverage of the issue is in his widely praised book, *Unspeakable Acts, Ordinary People: The Dynamics of Torture* (Knopf, 2000) and the *Chicago Reader's* John Conroy Archive at **ChicagoReader.com/PoliceTorture**. Conroy is the author of *Belfast Diary: War as a Way of Life* (Beacon Press, 1987, 1995). He has written for the *Chicago Tribune, New York Times, Washington Post, Boston Globe, Atlanta Journal-Constitution, Dallas Morning News, GQ, Mother Jones Granta* and many other publications, and has won numerous awards for his journalism. He now teaches investigation in the DePaul University College of Law and is a member of the TimeLine Theatre Writers Collective. **www.John-Conroy.com**

ALSO AVAILABLE FROM
CHICAGO DRAMAWORKS:

ACTION PHILOSOPHERS! By Crystal Skillman. Based on the award-winning, best-selling comic book series! Witness the lives and thoughts of history's A-list brain trust leap to the stage in manic, hilarious fashion. "Totally irreverent and manically inventive!" Publishers Weekly.

THE BEAR SUIT OF HAPPINESS by Evan Linder. In 1943, Woody, a young gay American, enlists in the army. After being shipped out to a remote Pacific Island, he is given an order: "Put up a show to entertain the men. Keep it simple. Needs music. And they like drag." Theatre of war and theatre of the mind play out together on Woody's little stage as he battles to build an identity and to be free. "This is a piece that stays with you." Chris Jones, Chicago Tribune.

BETWEEN by Michael Yichao. When Taylor arrives at yet another new foster home, he just wants time to find some sense of normalcy. But life works in strange ways, and his life and the lives of three other kids, each dealing with their own challenges and surprises, are about to cross in unexpected ways. They navigate the space between: between being a kid and being responsible, between what we want and what we get, between memory and future. A new play by Michael Yichao, *Between* examines the challenges of growing up, the relationships between adults and kids, and the strength young people find and lend to those around them.

PULP by Patricia Kane. July 1956. A hot and humid Chicago. Enter Terry Logan—tough-talking, rebellious, seductive. When she takes up residence at The Well, a club run by women who love women, the trouble really begins. Nominated for four Joseph Jefferson Awards including Best New Work, *Pulp* is a heartfelt, comedic love letter to lesbian pulp fiction and the Barbara Stanwycks of the world. "Fast and sassy. Pure entertainment!" - Theatremania.

For scripts and performance royalties, visit
www.ChicagoDramaworks.com

ALSO AVAILABLE FROM
CHICAGO DRAMAWORKS:

THE TAMING OF THE SHREW by Carin Silkaitis. Hotly debated for its jaw-dropping representations of sex, gender and power, William Shakespeare's *The Taming of the Shrew* has been inspiring controversy for centuries. This gender-bending adaptation by Carin Silkaitis is set in modern Brooklyn, and asks...*who's in control? Is anyone being tamed at all?*

TWELFTH NIGHT OF THE LIVING DEAD by Bryan Renaud. This bloody, over-the-top comedy combines original material with text from *Twelfth Night* and *Night of the Living Dead* to explore what happens when a zombie apocalypse plagues a production of one of the bard's funniest comedies. Join the cast on stage and off as they attempt to survive - without letting the audience know what's happening! A throwback farce with surprising poignancy, *Twelfth Night of the Living Dead* puts "the show must go on" to the test

UNSHELVED by Beth Kander. *On what - or whom - does your own identity depend?* When the matriarch of a seemingly normal family is diagnosed with early-onset Alzheimer's disease, the calm family picture begins to blur. Before her illness, Audrey had always protected her son and husband; now, as she sinks into the past, she reveals long-buried family secrets.

THE VANISHED by Barbara Lhota. Set in 16th-century Spain, *The Vanished* explores the impact of family ties, societal pressures and unexpected love through the story of two sisters. Featuring clandestine trysts, blackmail and swordplay, *The Vanished* is a thrilling romance with something for everyone. "Infused with drama, emotion and surprising twists, *The Vanished* delivers not only rough-and-tumble entertainment, but enough intrigue and romance to rivet the most avid soap opera fans. With clever, witty dialogue and vigorous swordplay, the play makes for a thoroughly enjoyable time." -Elena Ferrarin, Daily Herald

For scripts and performance royalties, visit
www.ChicagoDramaworks.com

Made in the USA
Monee, IL
18 November 2019

17023018R00075